The Lithuanian Crusade 1283–1435

COMBAT

Teutonic Knight
VERSUS
Lithuanian Warrior

Mark Galeotti

Illustrated by Giuseppe Rava

OSPREY PUBLISHING
Bloomsbury Publishing Plc
Kemp House, Chawley Park, Cumnor Hill, Oxford OX2 9PH, UK
29 Earlsfort Terrace, Dublin 2, Ireland
1385 Broadway, 5th Floor, New York, NY 10018, USA
E-mail: info@ospreypublishing.com
www.ospreypublishing.com

OSPREY is a trademark of Osprey Publishing Ltd

First published in Great Britain in 2023

A catalogue record for this book is available from the British Library.

ISBN: PB 9781472851505; eBook 9781472851512;
ePDF 9781472851499; XML 9781472851482

23 24 25 26 27   10 9 8 7 6 5 4 3 2 1

Maps by www.bounford.com
Index by Rob Munro
Typeset by PDQ Digital Media Solutions, Bungay, UK
Printed and bound in India by Replika Press Private Ltd.

Osprey Publishing supports the Woodland Trust, the UK's leading woodland conservation charity.

To find out more about our authors and books visit **www.ospreypublishing.com**. Here you will find extracts, author interviews, details of forthcoming events and the option to sign up for our newsletter.

Author's note

Although it is sometimes ungainly, place names of locations are generally given in both German and Lithuanian or Polish forms, where the names used at the time differ from the names used today. For the Lithuanian region of Žemaitija, the term Samogitia and Samogitians is generally used for the territory and people while they were under the rule of the Teutonic Order. The *Chronik des Landes Preussen* (*Chronicle of the Prussian Lands*) was originally written by Johann von Posilge. After his death in 1405, unknown collaborators continued the *Chronicle* until 1420, although for convenience henceforth von Posilge is cited in this study.

Artist's note

Readers may care to note that the original paintings from which the colour plates in this book were prepared are available for private sale. All reproduction copyright whatsoever is retained by the publishers. All enquiries should be addressed to:

info@g-rava.it

The publishers regret that they can enter into no correspondence upon this matter.

CONTENTS

Introduction

The crusade waged in the 13th and 14th centuries by the Teutonic Knights against Lithuania, the so-called 'last pagan land in Europe', witnessed bitter pitched battles, murderous treachery, gruelling sieges, economic statecraft and lightning raids. The Teutonic Knights were a rigidly authoritarian and brutally effective crusading order committed to spreading Christendom eastwards into the pagan realms of the Baltic and Russia. Their crusades were as much wars of colonization and enrichment, however, and with their allies, the Livonian Order, they prospered by the steady expansion of their lands. At the beginning of the 12th century, they had progressively extended their control across the various feuding tribes of Prussia and the Baltic – until they met the Lithuanians.

According to the 14th-century German chronicler Nicolaus von Jeroschin in *The Chronicle of Prussia*, it was in 1283 that the Teutonic Order ('the Order') started to wage war upon the Lithuanians (Fischer 2010: 208), and *Oberster Marschall* (Supreme Marshal) Konrad von Tierberg led a winter attack across the frozen Nemunas (Memel) River. In what may have been an inspiration to the famous – but wholly fictional – scene in Sergei Eisenstein's 1938 film *Alexander Nevsky* in which a Teutonic army falls through cracking ice into Lake Peipus, four fully armoured knights and one servant fell through the ice while crossing the river. Von Tierberg besieged the castle of Bisenė (near modern-day Jurbarkas, Lithuania), which he took after a hard siege, seized prisoners and plundered and laid waste to the surrounding farmland (Fischer 2010: 209). This set the pattern, and from the 1290s, the Teutonic Order launched several incursions into Lithuania each year.

Lithuania was not just some tribal land, however, but an increasingly ordered state. Unlike the Prussians and other opponents of the Teutonic Order, the Grand Duchy of Lithuania was a relatively well-organized and coherent polity. Its warriors could take advantage of the rough terrain

and thick woods of their native land, but would also learn invaluable lessons from both the mounted chivalry of the West and also the Mongols of the East. The Ordensstaat, the Order's autonomous state, saw this as a challenge to their economic as well as political and military status, in what was becoming the focus of their activities. Against the Lithuanians, the Order launched regular raids known as *Reisen*, 'journeys', slaughtering and burning as they went. They even developed this into what could be considered 'war tourism', as knights from across Europe paid to join these raids, honing their skills, enjoying the thrill of the hunt and fulfilling their crusading obligations without the long, uncertain journey to the Holy Land.

In the early years of the conflict between the Lithuanians and the Teutonic Order, raids more than pitched battles were the norm, staged to raze settlements, seize loot and prisoners, devastate farmlands, spread fear, and reward and encourage their respective warriors; what was known as a *chevauchée* in much of Europe. In modern-day terminology, this was a scorched-earth struggle rooted in economic warfare, ethnic cleansing and terror as much as anything else. As the *Livländische Reimchronik* (*Livonian Rhymed Chronicle*) recounted of one typical raid into Lithuania: 'The army spent the night under the protection of Our Lord … Master Andreas, bold hero that he was, began the march with his entire army. They moved into Nalsen, where they killed the people with a free hand. They slaughtered them like cattle – men, women and children – and few of them were spared' (Meyer 1876: 39–40).

Re-enactors recreate the close-quarters hand-to-hand combat of the mêlée at the time of the Lithuanian Crusade. (Michal Fludra/ NurPhoto via Getty Images)

Of all the pagan tribes of the eastern Baltic, it was the Lithuanians who managed to form a more cohesive and organized state, eventually making them one of the key powers in the region. Lithuania was a land of forests, swamps, lakes and rivers, shielding the fertile lands of the Nemunas (Memel), Viliya (Neris) and Vilnia river basins. The power base of the dynasty which rose to become the Grand Dukes of Lithuania was the highlands of Aukštaitija, with the regions of Dzūkija to the south-east, Suvalkija to the south-west and the western lowlands of Žemaitija all gathered in their grasp over time. Nevertheless, power was still relatively diffuse and feudal, with each of the 21 counties having their own *kunigas*, very loosely translated as 'duke' but in many ways still closer to a tribal chieftain.

This document from the Landesmuseum Württemberg in Germany shows successive popes and Holy Roman Emperors granting lands and privileges to the Teutonic Order. (Fine Art Images/ Heritage Images/Getty Images)

Lasting for more than 220 years, the Baltic Crusades constituted one of the longest wars in European history. To the Lithuanians, the war against the Teutonic Order was a struggle for their survival, and although many at the time assumed that the Teutonic Knights would in due course close their mailed fist around these pagans' necks too, and force them into submission, ultimately it was the Order that would be broken in a war that lasted over a century. The three battles explored in depth in this book highlight the ways in which the conflict changed – and did not change – over time, such that the Lithuanians, with their new Polish allies, were ultimately able to break the armies of the Teutonic Knights, and impose a defeat from which they would never really recover.

Territories of the Teutonic Order
- 1309
- 1346
- 1402

✠ Fortress of the Teutonic Order
◻ Seat of the *Hochmeister*
◯ Seat of a *Landmeister*
Bishoprics and city of Riga in Livonia
Frontier of the Holy Roman Empire

The Grand Duchy of Lithuania
- 1230s
- 1263
- 1341

← Lithuanian advances

Reval
Wesenberg
Narva
ESTONIA
Lake Peipus
HIIUMAA
Pernau
Fellin
Dorpat (Tartu)
SAAREMAA
Arensburg
LIVONIA
Pskov
Windau
COURLAND
Lemsal
Wolmar
Groß-Roop
Wenden
Visby
GOTLAND
Goldingen
Riga
Kokenhusen
Grobin
1260
Mitau
ZEMGALE
Kreutzburg
Rossitten
Ludsen
ÖLAND
Baltic Sea
Dünaburg
Polotsk
Memel (Klaipėda)
SAMOGITIA
Ragnit
Nemunas
Königsberg
Pregel
Insterburg
Kaunas
Vilnius
Balga
Allenburg
Braunsberg
Danzig
Angerburg
Elbing
Minsk
PRUSSIA
Marienburg (Malbork)
Bartelstein
Heilsberg
Rhein
POMERELIA
Christburg
Hammerstein
Osterode
Gardinas
Schlochau
Ortelsburg
Tuchel
Rehden
1410
Neidenburg
Kulm
Strasburg
Thorn
Dobrin
Warta
Vistula
Poznań
Gniezno

N

0   100 miles
0   100km

The Opposing Sides

ORIGINS

The Teutonic Order

The origins of the Teutonic Knights – more formally, the Order of Brothers of the German House of Saint Mary in Jerusalem – were peaceable enough. The *Domus Theutonicorum* (German House) of 12th-century Jerusalem catered for the needs of German crusaders, traders and pilgrims. Jerusalem fell to Salah ad-Din (Saladin) in October 1187, but the notion of the *Domus Theutonicorum* lived on in a hospital established in 1190 by merchants from Lübeck and Bremen in Acre, known as the Hospital of St Mary of the German House in Jerusalem. It became the basis for a monastic order, which given the needs and priorities of the time, became a fully-fledged military order in 1192. Pope Celestine III charged it with combining the role of hospice brotherhood and crusading order, and it took inspiration from both the Knights Hospitaller and the Knights Templar. Increasingly, however, the martial role came to define the *Deutscher Orden* (Teutonic Order).

Like its peers, the Teutonic Order accumulated holdings in Europe as well as the Holy Land, and even before it was expelled by the Arab conquests, it had been actively engaged in forcible conversion of the pagan Prussians. The Prussian Crusade was an on-off series of raids, invasions and colonizations, with progress often illusory (as pagans, forcibly baptized, returned to their old ways as soon as they could), but anchored by the construction of a series of *Ordensburgen* (fortresses), which would become part of the architecture of Teutonic Order power.

Albrecht von Buxthoeven, bishop of Riga, was appointed by the Archbishop Hartwig II of Bremen to Christianize the Baltic countries in 1199, yet crucially it was in 1226 that the Teutonic Order was formally petitioned by Bishop Christian of Oliva to assist the Christian Poles under

This illustration shows Emperor Frederick II (r. 1220–50) taking farewell from members of the Teutonic Order in Marburg. Note the distinctive black eagle of the Order's banner. Brother Hermann von Salza, Grand Master of the Teutonic Order (1209–39), was a close friend and ally of Frederick II, who had made him a *Reichsfürst*, or Prince of the Empire. At the time, Frederick II was consumed with the Fifth Crusade (1217–21), but he appreciated that securing Prussia would also secure the Holy Roman Empire's flank. From von Salza's point of view, this would allow the Teutons, who had never accumulated the vast wealth of the older orders, to establish a new power base. (Bildagentur-online/Universal Images Group via Getty Images)

Duke Konrad I of Masovia, who was suffering badly in his own struggles with the pagan Prussians. In March 1226, Emperor Frederick II issued the Golden Bull of Rimini, endorsing the Order's mission and granting it the fief of Chełmno Land, or Culmerland, in central-northern Poland, as well as such territories as it conquered. This was to be the basis of the future Ordensstaat because in August 1234 Pope Gregory IX issued the Golden Bull of Rieti confirming its control of the lands it conquered, subject only to the authority of the Papacy.

The Prussian Crusade began in earnest. Between the 1230s and 1270s, the Teutonic Order prosecuted an often-vicious campaign of conquest and colonization, fighting alongside Polish and other Christian forces. Having started with only around 100 knights and sergeants in the expedition, by 1233, the Order could field 10,000 of its own and allied soldiers. Prussian towns and tribes fell one by one, leading to a squabble over lands between Bishop Christian and the Order, which led to the latter being granted two-thirds of the territories seized. As they incorporated lands into the Ordensstaat, they also began to swallow up smaller crusading orders: first the Order of Dobrzyń and then the Livonian Brothers of the Sword, who became simply the Livonian Order, after their defeat at the hands of pagan Samogitian Lithuanians at the battle of Saulė on 22 September 1236.

By the end of the 13th century, Prussia was firmly defeated; at the same time, the Kingdom of Jerusalem finally and conclusively had fallen and the

A *Ritterbruder* ('Knight-brother') from the personal retinue of Grand Master Ulrich von Jungingen charging into battle at Grunwald. It is halfway through the battle, but the first time that the Grand Master himself leads his forces into battle, so the Knight-brother is enthusiastic, his destrier is fresh, and his armour and shield are undamaged. The knights of 16 full banners smash into the flank of the Polish army, but they fail in their initial objective of killing Jogaila and become pinned down in the mêlée, leaving them vulnerable to returning Lithuanian forces, which are able to engage them in both flank and rear. Von Jungingen will fall in battle, as will the original banner-bearer, and a second knight who then took his place.

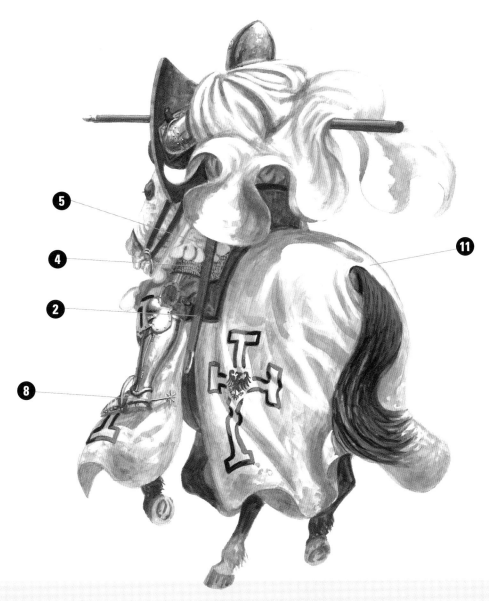

Weapons, dress and equipment

In the charge, the knight's lance (**1**) is a formidable weapon, but will likely soon break or be lost, so he also bears a long sword (**2**) on his left hip. His shield (**3**) bears the Teutonic Order's arms of a black cross and a *Reichsadler* (Imperial eagle) deriving from the Holy Roman Empire.

In coming decades, knights would increasingly adopt full plate armour, but his equipment reflects a transitional moment between 14th- and 15th-century standards. His full suit of mail consists of a thigh-length hauberk (**4**) with a coif, under a white surcoat (**5**) displaying the distinctive cross of the Teutonic Order. Over it, he has plate arm vambraces (**6**), cuisses and greaves (**7**) on his legs,

sabatons (**8**) on his feet and 'hourglass' gauntlets (**9**) on his hands. The 'pig-snout' visor of his bascinet helmet (**10**) would be worn hinged up to leave his face exposed for as long as possible, given how stuffy the closed helmet was and how far the visor obscured his vision, although it is now closed for battle.

His warhorse is unarmoured, as was still the usual practice at that time, but with an ornate white caparison (**11**) and a slightly dated wood-and-leather war saddle (**12**) – much less elegant than the parade seats used in other circumstances, but with a solid cantle better suited to absorbing the impact of a charge and keeping the knight on the horse.

focus of the Teutonic Order moved to the Ordensstaat. In 1309, after a brief period in which the Order was headquartered in Venice, Grand Master Siegfried von Feuchtwangen moved his seat to the imposing Ordensburg Marienburg (Malbork Castle) in Pomesania, a conquered Prussian tribal land north of Culmerland. In the process, as Teutonic rule moved eastward along the Baltic coastline, it would increasingly come into contact and then contention with the last and most coherent and powerful of the remaining pagan states: the Grand Duchy of Lithuania.

The Lithuanians

The first reference to Lithuania is found in the *Quedlinburger Annalen* (*Annals of Quedlinburg*), written between 1008 and 1030, which has an entry for 1009 mentioning the 'Litua'. Later Slavic chronicles mention it as a land raided by the Rus' and for a while forced to pay tribute to the principality of Polotsk, which would in turn become a Lithuanian dependency.

By the time the Lithuanians truly came to encounter the Teutonic Order, they had only recently been united, by conquest and alliance, during the reign of Grand Duke, later King, Mindaugas (r. 1236–53; king 1253–63), originally one of five regional rulers. Determined to prevail over his rivals, Mindaugas promised to convert to Christianity and surrender some land to the west in return for an alliance with the Livonian Order. He duly underwent baptism in 1251, and Pope Innocent IV recognized him as king of Lithuania.

Couronnement de Mendog Roi des Lithuaniens (1252). *Imp.r de Lacour*

After Mindaugas had won, he strove to expand his realm into the lands of the Rus', forcing Polotsk, which once had extorted tribute from the Lithuanians, to bend the knee. Meanwhile, the Livonian Order managed to use the opportunity to restore their fortunes to a degree and extend their territories in Žemaitija (known as Samogitia by the crusaders). Mindaugas, however, repudiated his treaty with the Livonians and, indeed, his conversion of convenience, which had never sat well with his pagan subjects. In the process, he formally lost his papal dispensation to kingship, and his successors would again be known as Grand Dukes.

The murder of Mindaugas in 1263 sparked a time of chaos and civil war. His fiery nephew Treniota seized the Lithuanian throne, only to be toppled by Mindaugas's son Vaišvilkas, a year later. A devout Christian, within three years Vaišvilkas had returned to monastic life – possibly under pressure – and was succeeded by his ally, Švarnas, an ambitious son of Daniel of Galicia. Švarnas in turn was killed in 1269, to be replaced by Traidenis, Duke of Kernavė.

A determined and effective leader, Traidenis defeated the Galicians and took to the field against the Livonian Order on multiple occasions, being responsible for the deaths in battle of not one but three Masters of the Livonian Order – Otto von Lutterberg, Andreas von Westfalen and Ernst von Rassburg – although the tales that he killed them personally are almost certainly poetic licence. When the Semigallians appealed to him for liberation from the Livonian Order, he led an army into the field, but died of natural causes in 1282, before he could make much headway.

Traidenis's successor, Daumantas, instead thought to raid and conquer again in the lands of the Rus', but died in battle in 1285 while attacking the

The coronation of Mindaugas as king of Lithuania on 6 July 1253. The armour depicted here is hopelessly anachronistic, but what this later illustration does convey is the way that the coronation (by papal bull, as part of Mindaugas's 'conversion' to Christianity) seems to have been carried out in the presence of just a few of his *leičiai*, or trusted armed retainers, presumably because of the risk of inflaming the anger of his predominantly pagan people. (Unknown/Wikimedia/Public Domain)

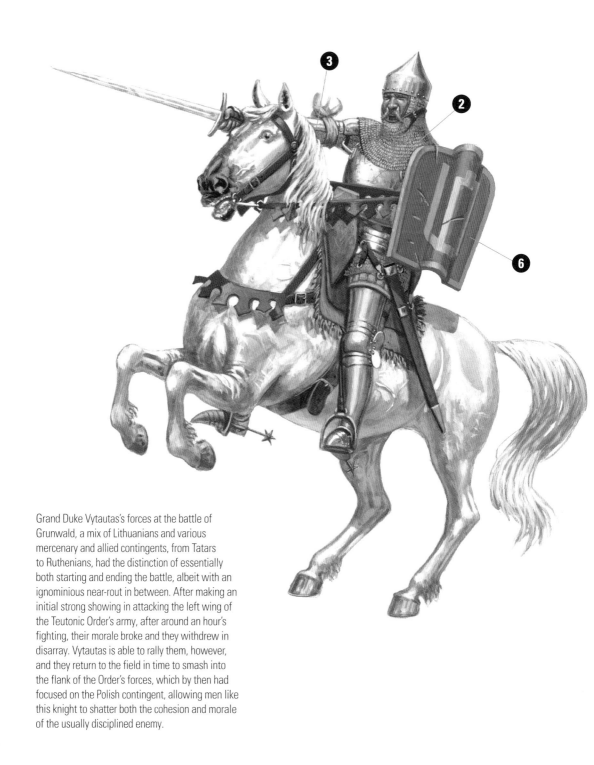

Grand Duke Vytautas's forces at the battle of Grunwald, a mix of Lithuanians and various mercenary and allied contingents, from Tatars to Ruthenians, had the distinction of essentially both starting and ending the battle, albeit with an ignominious near-rout in between. After making an initial strong showing in attacking the left wing of the Teutonic Order's army, after around an hour's fighting, their morale broke and they withdrew in disarray. Vytautas is able to rally them, however, and they return to the field in time to smash into the flank of the Order's forces, which by then had focused on the Polish contingent, allowing men like this knight to shatter both the cohesion and morale of the usually disciplined enemy.

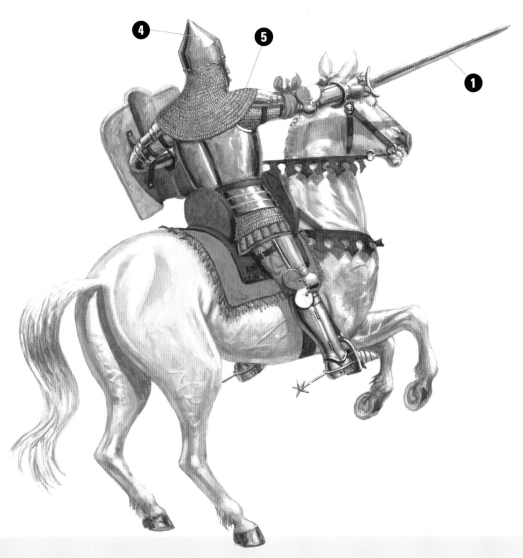

Weapons, dress and equipment

During the 15th century, Lithuanian knights would increasingly come to resemble their Western European counterparts, but this knight still displays some of the distinctive characteristics of Lithuania's warriors, including the helmet and shield style, bearing the so-called 'Pillars of Gediminas', the symbol of the ruling Gedimid dynasty since the late 14th century.

This knight would have borne a lance or spear into battle, but now that it has been presumably broken or discarded in close mêlée, he wields a long, straight sword (**1**). Whereas even by this time, some Lithuanian knights were still wearing lamellar or scale mail, he wears breastplate (**2**) and leg and arm armour, denoting his higher status. Around one of the straps fastening his rerebrace (**3**) to his upper arm is tied a lady's favour – while many of the mannerisms of courtly

chivalric behaviour found little traction in the Baltic region, clearly this custom did spread. Although most knights by this time were adopting helmets fitted with visors, sometimes attached to helms of the traditional Lithuanian design, he wears an old-fashioned helmet (**4**), over a mail coif (**5**). This same traditionalism is evident in his shield (**6**), the distinctive pavise-style design, with rounded edges and a protruding central pillar. This was really intended for infantry; most horsemen were replacing it with small, triangular kite shields.

Although some knightly mounts would wear full mail, this was often regarded as too exhausting, especially given the Lithuanians' preference for mobility over the single, heavy charge. Thus, they were typically unarmoured, as here.

city of Tver. With his death and the elevation of Grand Duke Butigeidis in 1285, Lithuania passed into the hands of the Gedimid dynasty, which would reign over the country for over a century. Butigeidis and his successor Butvydas ruled but briefly, however, so instead it was Butvydas's son Vytenis who truly stamped his dynasty's mark on the country during his reign of 1295–1316. A shrewd politician and a powerful war leader, Vytenis regained lands lost to the east and even managed to seal an alliance in 1297 with the Christian trading city and archbishopric of Riga, which was at daggers drawn by then with the Livonian Order, and he was able to use Riga as a base to launch raids into Prussia. The Lithuanians' raids were no less indiscriminate and devastating than those carried out by their opponents. Over time, they would get larger, and Grand Duke Vytenis's ultimately disastrous raid of 1311 that culminated on a wooded hilltop near the village of Voplaukis was an example of a rather more grandiose expedition.

Depicted in this rather crude 18th-century image, Mindaugas's fiery nephew Treniota emerged as a champion of paganism and expansionism. He had goaded his uncle Mindaugas into the demonstrative break with Christendom and had ambitions of uniting the pagan tribes of the Baltic. According to the *Livonian Rhymed Chronicle*, the ageing Mindaugas was not looking for a major war, and was unhappy that Treniota was not seeking to make alliances, which seemed to make the younger firebrand all the more impatient (Meyer 1876: 30). In any case, Mindaugas's fate would be sealed when his wife Morta died in 1262 and he chose to wed her sister (name unknown) in her place. Morta's sister was already married to Daumantas, *kunigas* of Nalšėnai, however, and so Daumantas threw in his lot with Treniota, and murdered Mindaugas in 1263. (Historic Images/Alamy Stock Photo)

RECRUITMENT AND MOTIVATION

The Teutonic Order

The Teutonic Order was imbued with a pervasive narrative that framed the pagans – often known as 'Saracens' – as somehow both subhuman and also actively hostile to Christianity. For example, the Teutonic Knights' own chronicler Peter of Dusburg, in his 1325 *Chronicon terrae Prussiae* (*Chronicle of the Prussian Lands*), asserted that the Lithuanians had their own pagan 'pope' in direct and blasphemous opposition to the true Pope of Rome (Urban 2003: 45). This was untrue, but helped justify the Teutonic Knights' methods and inspire the pious, attracting a continual stream of German aristocrats – typically younger sons who would not inherit their fathers' positions – to the Order and its harsh, monastic code.

The Holy Lands had long attracted European knights seeking glory or pardon from their sins, but for some, the time and hardship involved in a journey all that way was less appealing. To this end, the Baltic Crusades provided the same opportunities, albeit closer to hand. When the Holy Lands conclusively fell, north-eastern Europe became the main destination of would-be crusaders. The Teutonic Order capitalized on this demand with entrepreneurial enthusiasm. With the full blessing of the church, they organized for these so-called 'guest knights' regular *Reisen* raids on the 'Saracens'. These became increasingly organized and regularized, typically with two main raids a year, one in winter (leaving on Candlemass, 2 February) and one in summer (launched on the Day of the Assumption of Mary, 15 August). Depending on their success and supplies, *Reisen* could last from a fortnight to several months, and provided opportunities for young knights to practise their trade and win glory, burning, plundering and killing across pagan territories. The guest knights would pay for the privilege, and often also substantial sums for feasting before and after a *Reise*. Thus, the Order gained both additional military muscle and also profit. The Lithuanian lands would prove harder targets, however, and once they became Christian, then the rationale for the raids declined, even though by the time of the battle of Grunwald in 1410 there were still some willing to turn a blind eye to this fact in the name of a fight. That does, however, illustrate one problem with this model of attracting additional knights: they tended to be undisciplined, eager for a fight and unwilling to take orders. Indeed, they often saw themselves as high-paying customers 'on tour' as much as holy warriors under duty. When Henry Bolingbroke, earl of Derby and the future King Henry IV of England (r. 1399–1413), joined a *Reise* in 1390, for example, the total cost – which included travel to Prussia, and all ancillary costs – was fully £4,000, a huge sum that was paid by his father, John of Gaunt.

Those who were perhaps not able to commit to the full code, or who otherwise were not yet full brothers could become *Halbbrüder* ('Half-brothers'), also known as *Graumantler* (Greymantles) because they could not wear the pure white vestments of the full Teutonic Knights. Then there were the *Diener* (servants), who despite their name, also made up the Teutonic Order's infantry. It is also important to note, however, that the majority of most of the armies raised by the Ordensstaat were not made up of members of the Order but levies, mercenaries and also their 'guests' from across Europe – knights who had chosen to join the Lithuanian Crusade for one or more seasons or raids out of faith, martial enthusiasm or a desire to expunge past sins.

In Ordensstaat lands and affiliated territories such as the four bishoprics of the region and personal holdings of local German nobles, forces were raised on the basis of service obligations reflecting property ownership. Prussian freemen, after conquest and Christianization, would serve in the Teutonic Order's armies. Anyone holding land equal to a small farm or greater was subject to a duty of service, while others were simply hired for a campaign, for example, and typically fought as light infantry or cavalry. Conversely, German landowners holding more than 40 hides (672 hectares) of land had to serve as armoured knights. They were expected to provide their own weapons, armour and a warhorse, and had to be accompanied by at least two more horsemen and adequate remounts. Finally, the Ordensstaat would often field mercenaries from further afield. The famed Genoese crossbowmen were much prized, and were recruited for use in a number of battles, including the

Konrad von Thüringen, also known as Konrad Raspe, was the youngest son of Hermann I, Landgrave of Thuringia and Sophia, a daughter of Otto I, Duke of Bavaria. Von Thüringen was the first major aristocrat to join the Teutonic Order, reflecting its own increasing stature, and rose to the rank of Grand Master in 1239. (Bildagentur-online/Universal Images Group via Getty Images)

1390 siege of Vilnius. In addition, knights, cavalry and infantry from a range of other realms such as Bohemia and Masovia would also fight alongside the Order at various times, their Christian zeal reinforced by substantial payments.

The Lithuanians

The Grand Duchy of Lithuania was in many ways a rough-and-ready mix of European feudalism and traditional tribalism. The office of Grand Duke became increasingly regularized over time, but was originally little more than a warlord, who ruled over his noblemen and their warriors because he was able to win battles and earn them plunder. Every *bajoras* or *kunigas* (very broadly analogous to local gentry and dukes) had his own retinues of warriors, as did the Grand Duke himself. The *bajoras* would rule a number of villages, and recruit some of the more substantial peasants as well as his kin, sometimes equipping them at his own expense, otherwise expecting them to provide their own arms and armour. How many he recruited would depend on his resources, his martial zeal, his popularity, and the threats and opportunities of the season. The Grand Duke had his own trusted retinue, the *leičiai*, who were in their own way similar to the European knightly class, with their duties largely revolving around enforcing the authority of their lords and preparing for and waging war.

Lithuanian commoners were essentially civilians, but the strong raiding tradition within their society, and then the depredations of the crusaders, meant that they did more than their fair share of fighting, too, whether in the attack or the defence, as the supply of cattle, slaves and silver that they could seize was often crucial to the local economy. As such, they learned their combat skills in action and proved to be motivated to the point of ferocity in battle.

One of the founding fathers of the Lithuanian nation, Gediminas eztablished the city of Vilnius and is now commemorated by an impressive statue in the city's Cathedral Square. (Vladislav Gubarev/Wikimedia/ CC BY 3.0)

LEADERSHIP AND COMMUNICATIONS

The Teutonic Order

In theory, the Teutonic Knights operated within a rigid military–monastic structure, defined by its rules and organization. In practice, however, the realities of a dispersed structure in an age of poor communications, the habits and code of the feudal knightly elite and the presence of substantial numbers of foreign crusaders there for a year or a season inevitably meant that command and control was often less formal and correct than it should.

Organizationally, the Teutonic Order was led by the *Hochmeister* (Grand Master), who was elected for life. A General Council brought together representatives from each of the *Ballei* (bailiwicks), and the six

Senior figures within the Teutonic Order were not simply brother-knights but also members of the German aristocracy. This page from the *Wappenbuch des St. Galler Abtes Ulrich Rösch* (*Book of Coats of Arms of Ulrich Rösch, Abbot of St Gallen*) shows both the arms of the Grand Master of the Teutonic Order at the centre, and the personal arms of successive holders of the office, including Hermann von Salza (fourth on the top row). (Unknown/Wikimedia/Public Domain)

senior officers: Grand Master, *Grosskomtur* (Grand Commander), *Oberster Marschall* (Supreme Marshal), *Oberster Spittler* (Supreme Hospitaller), *Tressler* (Treasurer) and *Oberster Trappier* (Supreme Draper), the last of whom was responsible for maintaining the standards of dress and thus, by extension, the proper standards of the Order. Geographically, each province of the Ordensstaat was governed by a *Landmeister* (Land Master), who in turn administered various *Komtureis* (Commanderies), each under a *Komtur* (Commander). With the incorporation of the Livonian Order in 1243, their Master was also a *Vizelandmeister* (Deputy Governor) of the Ordensstaat.

This was an essentially administrative structure. On the battlefield, the *Komtur* was often the basic operational commander. He would typically lead a 'convent' of 12 full knights, as well as a contingent of half-brothers, militia, local levies and mercenaries expected to form a 'banner' at least 100 strong. In larger engagements, overall command could be in the hands of a *Komtur*, the *Oberster Marschall*, or even the *Hochmeister* himself.

The Lithuanians

As befitted its rough-and-ready mix of European feudalism and traditional tribalism, the organization of Lithuanian military forces was relatively personalistic. The position of Grand Duke may have been a hereditary one, but (as it was with any feudal ruler) his real power was limited by his relationship with his *kunigai*, who were still at heart the old chieftains of pre-unification Lithuania. The *kunigai*, in turn, depended upon the *bajorai*, the local chiefs. These positions were all notionally hereditary, although subject to disputes over rightful claim and precedence, and a Grand Duke would sometimes seek to elevate his own candidate if the opportunity arose, but above all would use the opportunity of territorial conquest to create new *bajorai* of his supporters.

An aggressive and charismatic Lithuanian ruler, Grand Duke Vytenis was not only an exemplar of his culture's raiding traditions, he also appears to have had a very personal hostility to Christianity, and together these led to his overreach that saw him brought to bay at Voplaukis. (The History Collection/Alamy Stock Photo)

A *bajoras* had his own personal retinue, but for war and raids would raise levies and volunteers from his own peasants, who fought both out of obligation and also the promise of loot. The basic building blocks of a Lithuanian army would thus be much more varied in size and nature than the Teutonic Order's as they reflected – depending on the scale of an action – the resources of a *bajoras* or *kunigas*. Forces from the highlands of Aukštaitija, for example, showed more influence from the Rus', including the presence of Rus' and Mongol-Tatar mercenaries, while those from the beleaguered Žemaitija lowlands, which faced the bulk of the Order's raids, were known for larger blocks of infantry and archers.

WEAPONS, ARMOUR AND HORSES

The Teutonic Order

In many ways the signature weapons of the Teutonic Order were the lance and sword of the knights, and the crossbows of their footmen. The lance, of course, was a symbol of chivalric aristocracy and valour, as well as a supremely effective weapon when wielded by an armoured knight on a galloping warhorse, able to focus all the weight of man and mount into a single point. After the first charge, knights would often be embroiled in the mêlée, and while the sword was the common close-quarters weapon, the mace and the axe were also favoured.

Footmen might be armed with spears or a variety of polearms, but like other Western medieval armies, the Teutonic Order also made wide use of crossbows, largely preferring them to regular bows (although they did deploy archers drawn from levy and allied or mercenary forces). The Order had several workshops which turned out both relatively advanced composite 'horn-bow' crossbows and the huge number of crossbow bolts that were needed. The 1139 Second Lateran Council had banned crossbows as 'deadly and hated by God' – primarily because they proved to be a great equalizer that would allow even commoners to kill heavily armoured military aristocrats – but this was only against Christians. Thus, crossbows were extensively used during the Baltic Crusades against the 'Saracens' and 'heathens'.

By the 15th century, crossbows used by the Teutonic Order were often fitted with a steel bow, and needed to be drawn with a windlass or ratchet winder because their draw weight had increased from around 150kg to near

These heads of arrows or crossbow bolts are preserved at the LWL-Museum für Archäologie in the Westfälisches Landesmuseum in Herne, Germany. (Markus Matzel/ullstein bild via Getty Images)

500kg. This gave them both greater range and power, and at the start of a battle they were used as indirect-fire weapons. A hail of shots fired diagonally upwards could rain down not just on the first rank of the enemy, but those behind, to a depth of some 200m. As well as regular bolts, crossbows would also fire *Heulbolzen* ('whistling bolts'), known to the Teutonic Order's crossbowmen as *Bremsen* ('gadflies'), which issued a sharp, whistling squeal on their flight, to demoralize and confuse the foe. Crossbows would then be used for direct fire at a range of up to 80m, with the bolts able to punch through armour and even shields.

The armour in use evolved over time, especially in the variety of forms worn by the knights. In the early 14th century, they still largely wore long coats of mail and heavy, restricting great helms, but these soon gave way to more flexible and protective ensembles of coats-of-plates over mail, and open-faced or visored bascinets. White vestments marked with the black cross of the Teutonic Order remained a constant. A half-brother might be just as well armoured, but would be attired in grey and, like servants' attire, only bore a black 'T' instead of a full cross on his apparel. Infantry might wear just a quilted gambeson, but over time also increasingly often wore mail, coats-of-plates and metal war-hats or similar simple helmets.

This early 14th-century illustration from the *Codex Manesse* shows a German crossbowman in what looks like a coat-of-plates, firing his crossbow upwards, demonstrating how the weapon could also be used for indirect fire. (Master of the Codex Manesse/Wikimedia/Public Domain)

Knights themselves would have carefully bred and tended warhorses, but they would conserve them for battle and instead ride saddle-horses on the march. Originally brought by the Teutonic Knights from their home territories such as Saxony and Thuringia, later warhorses were imported from Bavaria, the Rhineland or beyond and from the 14th century, the Teutonic Order bred its own in north-western Sambia. The Order also made growing use of a small local horse known as the Sweik, a breed indigenous to Lithuania and Prussia, for ancillary roles, from pack animals to couriers' mounts. In a letter of 1427, Grand Marshal Walrabe von Hunsbach praised these 'little shaggy horses' (quoted in Nicholson 1998: 122) that in many ways were every bit as crucial to the Order's military campaigns as the mighty destriers. A surviving document detailing the composition of an expedition to Kaunas (Kauen) in 1407, for example, listed 200 warhorses and saddle-horses, but fully 450–500 Sweiks to transport vital provisions and fodder in two-horse carts. Sweiks were also often ridden by Prussian auxiliaries, who would dismount before battle.

The Lithuanians

As a people between Western Europe and the lands of the Rus', the Lithuanians had a distinctive panoply of characteristic weapons and armour that showed influences from each. They were led by a mounted warrior class. While their forces tended to be lighter than the regular Ordensstaat forces, relying more on speed and agility than sheer mass, over time, the technological gap between Lithuanian and Teutonic Order forces would narrow sharply, especially when the former united with Poland in the 1385 Union of Krewo.

The Lithuanian forces used bows, but also often javelins, and over time first seized and later bought or made crossbows, too. In close combat, the spear, axe and sword were favoured, as well as the distinctive Lithuanian *sudlice*, a polearm similar to the *guisarme*, tipped by a long, broad, hooked spearhead. Whereas the *guisarme* was largely a foot soldier's weapon, the *sudlice* could also be wielded from horseback by experienced Lithuanian warriors, and like their infantry counterparts, they would often seek to use it to hook enemy riders from the saddle.

A Lithuanian warrior for most of the time of the Baltic Crusades would typically wear a coat of mail or scale and a distinctive brimmed conical helmet (also common among the Rus'). By the 15th century, however, the richest among them – especially the *leičiai* and the *kunigai* – were increasingly likely

The *sudlice*, a distinctively Lithuanian weapon, was a polearm with an axe-blade surmounted by a spike, often with a hook that could be used to unhorse enemy cavalry. (Rama/Wikimedia/ CC BY-SA 2.0 fr)

to be armed and armoured more like their Western counterparts. Indeed, a document compiled by the Teutonic Order to be delivered at the 1415 Council of Constance went so far as to complain that the Lithuanians wore metal armour and rode warhorses as if this were somehow unsporting (Nicholson 1998: 133).

Lithuanians had regular contact with Mongol-Tatar armies and emissaries, and like the Rus', they adopted some of their style of warfare, especially the use of fast-moving light cavalry for both skirmish and attack. The horsemen would typically ride the stocky and muscular little Sweik; but it was a mark of the growing convergence between Lithuanian and Teutonic equipment, and thus the way of war, that in the late 14th century there were already emerging reports that Kęstutis had set up a stud farm to breed warhorses, largely by plundering his initial breedstock from the Teutonic Order.

TRAINING AND TACTICS

The Teutonic Order

The nature of the Baltic Crusades shaped the tactics employed by the Teutonic Knights, honed over decades of warfare against the Prussians and others. Despite reversals such as the First Prussian Uprising of 1242 and the Great Prussian Uprising of 1260–74, the Teutonic Order had enjoyed the advantages of discipline, technology and its own network of fortifications. Although their heavily armed and armoured cavalry and the foot soldiers' crossbows were less effective in skirmishes in the forests, and many of their fortresses fell, the crusaders were able to count on divisions among the Prussians and other 'heathens', too. The Great Prussian Uprising, however, was a much more serious affair, sparked by the Samogitians' defeat of the Livonian Order at Skuodas (Schoden/

Skudn) in 1259, and then the Teutonic Order itself at Durbe (Durben) the next year. It would be a long, bitter struggle, and so unnerved were the crusaders that they adopted even harsher tactics, exterminating those who would not submit and convert, and forcibly resettling others or using them as conscript labour in the construction of imposing new fortresses with which to maintain their rule.

The Teutonic Order's troops trained and fought primarily in two types of operation, at opposite ends of the spectrum: launching or defending against the raids that were the norm, or occasional set-piece battles, often involving sieges. This in effect created a tension in their training: set-piece battles were best served by focusing on coordinated unit-level manoeuvres, while raids set great store on individual prowess. In practice, while the Teutonic Knights were relatively disciplined and thus able to make the best of their combined arms on the battlefield, the emphasis for most still lay on their personal skills.

Although on the larger battlefield the Teutonic Order relied on the crashing impact of the knights' charge, raids were often relatively small and conducted in terrain not at all conducive to such tactics. A hard winter would freeze the ground, permitting easy travel, for example, but deep snow, thick forests, boggy ground and similar conditions in many ways gave the advantage to the Lithuanian skirmishers and light cavalry, and forced the knights to depend on their crossbowmen and local auxiliaries to screen them.

The Teutonic Order was able to draw on the wider advances in Western European military siegecraft and engineering. In a siege, they would ideally seek to establish a *circumvallation*, their own palisades and defences right around the target, to deter or resist both sallies and relief. Engineers and conscripted labourers would divert streams that fed moats or fill them with earth, wood and rubble. They might undertake the risky task of trying to sap enemy walls, digging down to undermine their foundations, or else miners would push tunnels under the walls and then collapse them and, they hoped, the fortifications above. More aggressively, the Order would deploy a range of siege artillery: ballistae that fired huge arrows; and catapults and larger trebuchets, both of which could hurl stone balls or burning wads of pitch. At a crucial moment, walls might be stormed either by the simple expedient of long, wooden siege ladders or lumbering siege towers. Covered in planks, leather or even metal, these were intended to bring assault forces up to the top of the enemy walls. Meanwhile, battering rams would be deployed against gates and other weak spots. By the late 14th century, simple firearms – both crude 'hand-cannons' and larger siege weapons – were already beginning to come into use. Of course, the essence of arms races is that what one side uses, the other side can learn to use. Although the first reliable mention of the Order's guns is in a description of the use of bombards during a siege in 1338, only 20 years later, the Lithuanians were themselves using bombards against Teutonic Order castles.

The Lithuanians

A combination of a martial tradition, strong personal ties with their traditional leaders, a sense that they were defending not only their lands but their faith, and the lack of mercy shown by the crusaders ensured that Lithuanian warriors tended to be fierce in the attack and resolute in the defence.

These reconstructed trebuchets, photographed in 2019 at Nykøbing Falster in Denmark, convey the formidable size and range of these feared siege engines. (Ole Jensen/Getty Images)

The Lithuanians were a raiding culture, even before this became one of the primary forms of war with the Teutonic Order. Although there were limits as to how extensive or violent they could be, before the Grand Duke might have to step in, villages would often raid the villages of other *bajorai*, above all to steal livestock, and this provided a constant source of training for warriors and ordinary peasants alike. Furthermore, every *bajoras* or *kunigas* had his own retinues of warriors, as did the Grand Prince. They trained as assiduously as any Christian knight and also engaged in pursuits such as hunting and raiding that also honed necessary skills.

The Teutons made an early mistake when they assumed that Lithuanians were essentially the same as Prussians, with no central leadership or sense of order and discipline. They would come to realize that this was an error of judgement. Indeed, they even found opportunities to take advantage of it. The Teutonic Knights had observed, for example, that in the border forts which represented the Lithuanians' defensive front line, there was a strict rotation of garrisons. They would serve a month before being replaced and heading back home. This allowed for the ambush of garrisons leaving Bisenė, the westernmost of the forts. Until it was burned down by the Teutonic Knights in 1316, three times units leaving the fort were ambushed and largely wiped out by Teutonic Order forces that had managed to infiltrate Lithuanian territory.

MORALE AND LOGISTICS

The Teutonic Order

The modern reputation of the Brothers of the Teutonic Knights is as supremely disciplined fighters, in part because of their representation in Eisenstein's seminal film, *Alexander Nevsky*, in which their orderly, almost mechanical

ranks are contrasted with the organic, enthusiastic Russian forces for political as well as aesthetic purposes. There is some truth in the portrayal, but also a great deal of myth-making, and contemporary accounts paint a much more nuanced picture. Nevertheless, the Teutonic Knights' fervour and hunger for battle is unquestionable. As the *Livonian Rhymed Chronicle* puts it somewhat archly, 'they were burdened greatly with fighting, but endured it gladly for the sake of God' (Meyer 1876: 71). They often proved to be as determined in defeat as in victory, and were willing to conduct themselves in the most brutal ways in the name of a cause they felt was just and right.

Especially in the earlier years of the Prussian conquest, the Teutonic Knights had to maintain constant vigilance, as they would be more likely to fall victim to an opportunistic attack than a full-scale revolt or attack. According to the *Livonian Rhymed Chronicle*: 'They steadfastly propagated the True Faith, but this was often difficult. Whoever was careless and let down his guard could easily be killed. They endured many hardships: they kept watch, went hungry and thirsty, and seldom rested. Their sufferings were great' (Meyer 1876: 32). This nevertheless helped maintain their discipline and their sense of being a force wholly separate from the locals, and who needed to support and defend each other. Despite the usual challenges of discipline within the European military aristocracy, the Teutonic Knights, even more so than many other crusading orders, were known for their rigorous discipline and commitment to their monastic code. As a result, their morale was less dependent on the ebb and flow of victory and defeat, hardship and opportunity, than many other armies of the time. Although like any soldiers, they could be prone to overconfidence in the attack and being routed in defeat, their morale was relatively strong for most of this time, bolstered by their faith.

It was at once an asset and a vulnerability that the Teutonic Order was able to draw on 'pilgrims' like this Italian guest knight, as they often – as at the battle of Grunwald – proved much less disciplined than their monastic comrades. (Fine Art Images/Heritage Images/ Getty Images)

Teutonic Order logistics were also unusually well-organized by the standards of the time. There still survive records demonstrating how careful were the preparations especially for the larger variety of raid known as a *Hervart* ('offensive expedition'), for example, with food, fodder, spare clothing, shelter and ammunition all carefully allotted and accounted for, carried by pack-horses or sledges in winter, wagons in summer. Routes were planned in advance and stocks of food and fodder placed along the way, as far as possible.

The Lithuanians

The Lithuanians demonstrated themselves to be formidable fighters. Indeed, von Jeroschin, in *The Chronicle of Prussia*, described them as 'famously well-built, strong and daring, swift, courageous, bold, fierce and skilful at war,

because they practice continually from early childhood' (Fischer 2010: 208). Even allowing for a degree of hyperbole, because the more dangerous the enemy, the more impressive Teutonic victories would then appear, there must be some truth to this. Although more prone to buckle and break than the Teutonic Knights themselves, the Lithuanians in turn proved to be more disciplined and enthusiastic fighters than the other Teutonic Order troops, and tended to regroup quickly when they did retreat.

Furthermore, while the Lithuanians may have lacked the careful, bureaucratic approach to managing their logistics as did the Teutonic Order, in practice they did almost as well given their flexibility and their deep experience in raiding. They hunted and foraged well on the march, made do with limited supplies, and knew to bring adequate stocks of arrows and the other consumables of battle with them. Where they originally suffered was in their supplies of siege weapons and similar heavier equipment. Exposure to the Order and the increasing scale of their warfare meant that the Lithuanians learned quickly, however. As the role of the Grand Duke became increasingly institutionalized, and the power and wealth at his personal disposal increased, he acquired the resources and capability to assemble and field such weapons himself.

A modern recreation of the idol that would have been at the centre of an open-air shrine to Perkūs, the Baltic pagan god of storm, war and law. Although there were details in name and practices – Perkūs was known as Perkūnas to the Lithuanians, for example – the essence of the Baltic pagan beliefs was quite similar across tribes and cultures and also bore similarities to Nordic beliefs. (Šarūnas Šimkus-Kalvaitis/Wikimedia/Public Domain)

The Lithuanian pagan tradition known as Romuva includes such practices as a winter solstice celebration of burning the 'Blukis', a wooden stump that is dragged around a town, beaten and then burned, to represent the freeing of the sun to ensure the return of spring. (PETRAS MALUKAS/AFP via Getty Images)

Voplaukis

1311

BACKGROUND TO BATTLE

In 1298, Grand Duke Vytenis concluded a 15-year agreement with the city of Riga that to a large degree neutralized the threat he faced from the Livonian Order, including taking their castle at Karkus (Karksi) and killing their Master, Bruno, when he tried to launch a retaliatory attack. This allowed Vytenis to focus his attentions on Ordensstaat Prussia, which was itself launching raids across the Nemunas River. Part of his response was defensive, building and strengthening a chain of wooden forts along the Nemunas and Jūra rivers, which were matched by forts built by the Teutonic Knights on the opposite riverbanks.

Vytenis was not willing to stay on the defensive, however. As the Teutonic Order was seeking to push through Žemaitija, along the Baltic coastline, to link up with the Livonian Order, he carried out some 20 raids into Ordensstaat-held Samogitia to slow their advance, by burning forts and villages and deterring local leaders from throwing their lot in with the crusaders. Many of them seem to have been willing to be baptized and become vassals of the Order in order to avoid the worst of the Teutonic Knights' own depredations. Vytenis appears to have wanted them to realize that the dangers from changing sides could be even greater, however.

Having pledged at the start of 1311 to stage a grand expedition into Prussia, in mid-February, Vytenis marched his personal retinue from his capital, Vilnius, to Kaunas, where he had instructed a number of his *kunigai* to muster with their own forces. By 23 February, they were harrying the lands of the Sambians. Vytenis's aim was to rely on speed, surprise and savagery. He was not looking to fight a pitched battle, so he avoided the mighty Teutonic Order red-brick fortresses of Königsberg (Kaliningrad) and Brandenburg

(Ushakovo) and instead raided and looted at will, catching the Christians during the celebrations that marked Shrove Tuesday.

Vytenis then continued on into the lands of the conquered Warmian tribe, eventually reaching the fortified city of Braunsberg (Braniewo). Without a siege train, and aware that were he to pause too long, he would be vulnerable to encirclement by slower yet stronger Teutonic forces, Vytenis satisfied himself with burning the fields around Braunsberg's walls, killing the inhabitants and plundering the area, and taunting Bishop Eberhard of Warmia who stood on the city's walls (Fischer 2010: 257).

Insofar as one can gather from admittedly biased Christian accounts, there seems to have been a genuine and serious edge to Vytenis's hostility towards Christianity. While some other Grand Dukes treated the religious dimension of their wars as secondary to the political, Vytenis would often go out of his way to attack religious sites and communities. In 1294, for example, he had launched a substantial raid on the Polish town of Łęczyca (Lentschitza) during which, according to von Jeroschin, Vytenis burst into the cathedral and killed 400 people, going on deliberately to desecrate the contents of the building (Fischer 2010: 224).

In his *Chronica nova Prutenica* (*New Prussian Chronicle*), Teutonic Order herald and chronicler Wigand of Marburg claims that the attackers were trapped by Teutonic forces and defeated, but he is probably confusing this raid with Vytenis's second raid later the same year, which went rather less well for Vytenis (Hirsch 1863: 12). Instead, it is clear that the Lithuanians were able to withdraw before the Teutonic Order could concentrate its forces, this time plundering and burning their way across the lands of the Natangians as they headed home. Friedrich von Wildenberg, *Komtur* of Königsberg, led an unsuccessful attempt to intercept Vytenis's retreat, and in retaliation – and, one suspects, frustrated outrage – attacked and ravaged the border region of Pagraudė as a reprisal, killing, enslaving and looting with comparable abandon. Nevertheless, Vytenis must have regarded this expedition as an eminently satisfactory one, and it seems so too did his men, because when he incautiously decided to stage a repeat performance, many more *kunigai* and *bajorai* actively sought to join, eager for their share of the glory, slaves and plunder that seemed so plentiful and easy to win. Von Jeroschin is probably right to blame this on hubris, pointing out that Vytenis's long run of good fortune had made him so overconfident that he believed he could threaten anyone with impunity (Fischer 2010: 256).

Thus, on 3 April 1311, Vytenis launched a second, much larger raid on the lands of the Natangians. According to Peter of Dusburg, Vytenis's army numbered 4,000 men, a figure also reported by von Jeroschin in *The Chronicle of Prussia* (Fischer 2010: 256). Such numbers must be treated with considerable caution, but nevertheless, this was clearly a much larger expedition than Vytenis's earlier raid, and one with a greater proportion of infantry – something that would prove to have serious implications in the future.

Vytenis marched through the lands of the Natangians, burning villages and gathering prisoners and plunder on the way, and may have been planning to head through to the lands of the Pogesanians further to the west. Grand Commander Heinrich von Plötzke, the former *Landmeister* of Prussia, had

anticipated such a move, however, and had been ready to muster forces to block Vytenis's potential lines of retreat. Von Plötzke had left his personal seat at Elbing and established himself at Mohrungen (Morąg), from where he began to summon the *Komture* of the region.

Reports vary as to whether Vytenis received word of this development or simply had already gathered so much plunder from the Natangians that his army could haul no more, but either way he had already begun to prepare to return home when his scouts warned him that Teutonic Order forces were assembling to block his retreat. Vytenis realized that his army, loaded as it was with loot and heavily made up of slower foot soldiers, risked being caught between the anvil of the screening forces ahead and von Plötzke's hammer coming up behind. Vytenis was no coward and he had a substantial army behind him. It was time to fight, and he settled on a wooded hilltop near the village of Voplaukis as a suitable place to do battle.

The Teutonic Order's control of pagan lands was underpinned by a series of castles and fortified cities. This is the ruined East Bailey of Karkus Castle, a Teutonic Order *Ordensburg* (fortress) built on the site of a former Estonian hillfort in the 14th century. Such fortifications housed a chapter of knights and their servants, and also controlled key communications routes – in this case, the route between southern and northern Livonia. (Oscar.susi/ Wikimedia/CC BY-SA 3.0)

MAP KEY

1 Mid-February: Vytenis marches from Vilnius to Kaunas to muster his forces.

2 23 February: Lithuanian forces harry the lands of the Sambians.

3 28 February: Vytenis continues into the lands of the Warmians, even reaching Braunsberg, where although he is not able to besiege the city, he taunts Bishop Eberhard of Warmia.

4 2 March: Lithuanian forces turn back before a strong defence can be mustered, harrying the lands of the Natangians on their return route.

5 3 April: Vytenis launches a second, much larger raid into the lands of the Natangians, burning villages and gathering prisoners and plunder.

6 April: Anticipating such a move, Grand Commander Heinrich von Plötzke musters forces to block the Lithuanians' potential lines of retreat.

7 6 April: As Vytenis begins to head back, his scouts warn him of the Teutonic Order forces ahead, and he settles on a wooded hilltop at Voplaukis as a suitable place to do battle.

8 7 April: The Teutonic forces duly engage, first with a probing attack, then their full strength. Vytenis is able to flee, but his army is broken and routed.

Battlefield environment

The hilltop at Voplaukis was a broad, regular cone, at most some 12m in height, topped by a wide flat space that was partly covered by light scrubland, providing a good area for the Lithuanians to tether their horses. Otherwise, the top and slopes of the hill were wooded, and while the trees were not especially dense, they sufficed to impede a full uphill charge by mounted knights, especially as much of the space in between was chocked with bushes and undergrowth. The surrounding land was essentially wild, even though farmers from the nearby village of the same name were beginning to clear some of the land to the north-west of the hill for eventual cultivation.

Modern-day Wopławki. Time has tamed what was once a wooded and heavily undergrown land, and it is now distinctly more bucolic. The Teutonic Order had built a watch tower in the village, but it was apparently unmanned when the Lithuanians arrived and put it to the torch. It appears that the village itself was largely destroyed or abandoned as a consequence of the battle, and took more than 50 years to be repopulated. (Ralf Lotys/ Wikimedia/CC BY 3.0)

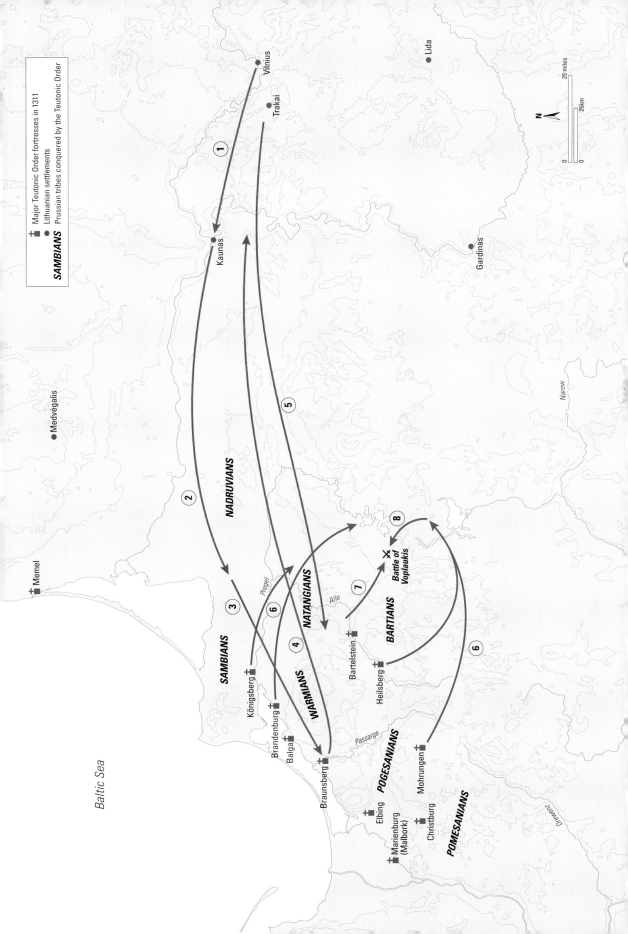

Baltic Sea

Memel

Medvégalis

Vilnius

Lida

Trakai

Kaunas

Gardinas

Narew

①

②

⑤

NADRUVIANS

③

⑥

④

⑧

Battle of
Voplaukis

⑦

NATANGIANS

Alle

Pregel

SAMBIANS

Königsberg

Brandenburg

Balga

Braunsberg

WARMIANS

Bartelstein

BARTIANS

Heilsberg

⑥

Passarge

POGESANIANS

Mohrungen

Elbing

Christburg

Marienburg
(Malbork)

POMESANIANS

Drewenz

SAMBIANS

+■ Major Teutonic Order fortresses in 1311
● Lithuanian settlements
● Prussian tribes conquered by the Teutonic Order

N

25 miles

25km

0

0

INTO COMBAT

On 6 April 1311, Vytenis's forces settled on a wooded hilltop near the village they called Voplaukis (now known as Wopławki and at the time called Woplauken by the Germans) and began preparing it for battle. Wagons bearing loot were drawn up to provide cover, and where the Lithuanians saw potential attack routes, they began setting up abatis defences. Trees were felled and sharp branches set into the ground or interlaced to form barriers. They lacked the time to surround the whole hill, however, and as night fell, settled into an uneasy rest.

The chroniclers' claims that Vytenis led a force of 4,000 warriors, and had also by this stage captured 1,200 (Peter of Dusburg) or 1,300 (Nikolaus von Jeroschin) prisoners are clearly inflated. Nevertheless, this was a substantial force, with a core of mounted warriors, including Vytenis's own retinue and those of several *kunigai*, a large force of Lithuanian foot soldiers, and auxiliaries and mercenaries including a force of Ruthenian – Rus' – soldiers. The ratio would seem to have been 20 per cent cavalry, 70 per cent Lithuanian infantry and 10 per cent mercenaries. Although von Jeroschin characterizes them as combat-tested veterans selected for their courage and military prowess (Fischer 2010: 256), in fact many were levies and young men who had joined the expedition precisely to learn the arts of raiding.

Vytenis's men had taken some losses, but in the main they were in relatively good condition for troops who had been in the field. The loot they were carrying limited their tactical options, however. Just as it imposed a tough choice on Vytenis – he might have been able to keep ahead of the crusaders had he been willing to abandon the prisoners and wagons and forced march eastwards – it also meant that part of the force was required to keep guard on the prisoners, because although the chroniclers tend to characterize them as all being female non-combatants held captive in chains (Fischer 2010: 257), in practice some would be young men intended to be sold as farm labour slaves. Furthermore, many units would not move far from their own wagons of plunder.

The chroniclers are on more solid ground when describing von Plötzke's force. The core comprised between 80 and 150 full knights, supported by both half-brothers and Prussian militia levies. Wigand of Marburg lists the separate banners that had been mustered: the commanderies of Ragnit, Insterburg, Christburg, St George, St Mary, and Prussian Holland (which was part of the Elbing district, under von Plötzke). Given that a typical banner was composed of around 100 fighting men, that implies a force of 600, of whom maybe one-sixth were full knights. The Teutonic Order's forces demonstrated the usual determination in battle for which they are known, but the Prussian levies proved of variable quality, some being unwilling to press home assaults into the face of a hail of Lithuanian javelins and arrows, while others demonstrated great ferocity in the attack.

The first banner to reach the battlefield the next morning was that led by Günther von Arnstein, *Komtur* of Christburg. Whether because of his orders or, more probably, excessive enthusiasm, von Arnstein immediately launched an attack up the hillside. The attack was prosecuted with typical zeal, but the vastly outnumbered Christians were met with a storm of arrows

Dating from the 14th century, this two-piece bascinet is missing its aventail, which would have been attached via riveted loops to the lower edge. The style is characteristic of the Teutonic Order. (INTERFOTO/Alamy Stock Photo)

and javelins so thick it looked like snow was falling (Fischer 2010: 258). Ruthenian archers and javelineers played a prominent role in blunting the initial assault. Although some of the attackers got part way up the slope, none seem to have been able to close with the defenders, before they were forced to retreat, leaving their casualties behind on the hillside. Von Jeroschin claims that they lost 40 men, Peter of Dusburg gives a figure of 60 – either way, it represented a serious butcher's bill, given that the walking wounded would have been able to withdraw.

Vytenis was reportedly cock-a-hoop, perhaps not appreciating that this was only a small part of the full Teutonic Order army mobilized against him. According to the Christian chroniclers, he taunted the retreating soldiers, asking them why their deity did not help the crusaders like his gods had assisted the Lithuanian cause during the recent fighting and previously (Fischer 2010: 257).

Meanwhile, however, the rest of the Teutonic Order's forces had arrived. Von Arnstein's quixotic initiative had suffered from being able to attack up

Von Arnstein attacks at Voplaukis, 1311

Order view: *Komtur* Günther von Arnstein has thrown his banner into an impetuous and ill-judged unsupported assault on the assembled Lithuanian forces, which have taken up positions on a wooded hilltop near Voplaukis. His men are a mix of Teutonic Knights and footmen, supported by Prussian levies, and they are beginning to waver under a storm of arrows and javelins from the defenders. The knights, while mounted and well-armoured, are not well-suited to such operations and their horses in particular are proving especially vulnerable. The knights' footmen, who bear the black tau instead of the black cross of full knights, are torn between pressing home the attack and supporting the brother-knights. As for the Prussians, while they are more primitively armoured, they are better suited to such an operation, but also notably less motivated.

Lithuanian view: Vytenis's men know they cannot retreat and thus must hold the hill and hope to break the Teutonic Order's will to try to contest it. At present, as they see the attackers' morale wavering, the Lithuanians are in good spirits, unaware that this is just a first and understrength assault. One of Vytenis's own mounted *leičiai* is encouraging the men on, the grizzled professional warrior's banner bearing a cross symbol that, confusingly, has pagan rather than Christian origins. Most are Lithuanians, although there is also a Ruthenian mercenary to the left of their line. They are equipped in classic Lithuanian style, especially with the distinctive eastern European conical helmet, and one spearman's shield displays the bear of Žemaitija.

only one side of the hill, allowing the defenders to concentrate their fire. Von Plötzke had sufficient forces at his disposal (and was an experienced enough commander) that he divided them, with two feints and a main assault. This compelled the Lithuanians to try to defend the whole perimeter of the hill, and allowed the main force, under von Plötzke, to punch through into the Lithuanian camp.

It was a hard-fought battle of sword against spear, but despite their advantage of numbers, the Lithuanians' morale broke. Von Arnstein, intent on redeeming his earlier failure, was the first to break through their defensive line, shocking them and prompting a noisy rout akin to the behaviour of startled starlings (Fischer 2010: 258). Vytenis himself, attended by his mounted retinue, managed to fight free and fled at full speed, abandoning loot, prisoners and the bulk of his army. Most of the horses were still corralled – the crusaders reportedly captured 2,800 of them, although this figure may be an exaggeration and would include those that had been taken by the Lithuanians as plunder – and so other knots of defenders had to try to make their escape on foot. Most would be ridden down as they fled, or were easy prey to the crusaders' crossbows or the bows of their Prussian auxiliaries.

As usual in battle, a retreat could become a rout, and a rout a massacre. At this stage, von Jeroschin's account becomes particularly animated, exhorting the crusaders to avenge the Christian lives lost, churches burned and non-

Built on the site of Tuwangste, a wooden Prussian fort near the Pregel (Pregolya) River, the Teutonic stronghold of Königsberg went from an initial wooden stockade to a stone castle and later a sprawling fortress used as a residence for the Grand Master of the Teutonic Order. This view dates back to the early 18th century; the castle itself was gutted by aerial bombing in World War II and later demolished by the Soviets. (Kupferstecher/ Wikimedia/Public Domain)

combatants mistreated, and glorying in the bloodshed inflicted upon the fleeing Lithuanians until they were all wiped out (Fischer 2010: 258). Their discipline broken, bereft of their leaders and stranded in hostile territory, the Lithuanians certainly suffered a terrible defeat. According to certain later Russian accounts, some Ruthenians were able to lie low and later make their way home, but this is quite possibly simply folk myth. The *Annales canonici Sambiensis* claim that, all told, the Lithuanians lost 3,000 men, and while this exact figure may be questionable, it does fit the overall sense that some three-quarters of their army was either killed or captured (Arndt 1866: 699). Either way, this was undoubtedly a crushing defeat for Vytenis whose greed and hubris in launching a second raid on the lands of the Natangians so soon after his first, and along such a similar trajectory, gave von Plötzke the perfect opportunity to take revenge for Vytenis's previous success.

Von Jeroschin somewhat overplays the significance of the Teutonic victory, claiming that the whole of Prussia's Christian population was thereby saved from persecution and slaughter (Fischer 2010: 259). It was, after all, just another raid, albeit an unusually large one. The real impact was on Lithuania. Although Vytenis was able to escape, this was a serious defeat for him, and he did not launch any more expeditions of comparable scale in the remaining years of his reign. These would be relatively peaceful years, not so much because of any outburst of amity but as a result of exhaustion and strategy. Although 1311 saw at least three more raids mounted by the Teutonic Order's forces as they sought to capitalize on their victory, they instead focused on preparations for more substantial power projection into Lithuania. In particular, Grand Master Karl von Trier decided that they would take advantage of a lull in Lithuanian raids to build Ordensburg Christmemel on the banks of the Nemunas River.

This was no easy feat, however, requiring as it did the construction of a bridge made of wooden boats lashed together to allow men and *matériel* to cross the river. Nevertheless, by the end of April 1313, the fortress had been built, with strong wooden walls atop earthen ramparts, and garrisoned with fully 400 knights and soldiers. Vytenis laid siege to Ordensburg Christmemel in September 1315, in a major attack that saw him deploy not just siege engines but also mercenary Russian archers. Nevertheless, after 17 days, as Teutonic reinforcements neared, Vytenis abandoned the attempt, his last military engagement before his death. As a result, the Teutonic Order was now truly entrenched on Lithuania's frontiers, and would seek in the future not simply to raid its border regions and harry its defenders, but to prepare for a serious campaign finally to bring these 'Saracens' to heel. It would not be easy, however.

This depiction of knights and musicians is at Malbork Castle, known as Ordensburg Marienburg to the Teutonic Order. (Mauricio Abreu/Alamy Stock Photo)

The Siege of Kaunas

1362

BACKGROUND TO BATTLE

The Lithuanian Crusade remained one fought largely through the raid, but these became increasingly extensive and well organized. Both the Teutonic Order and the Lithuanians were galvanized by the on-off war. The Lithuanians not only captured more advanced weapons and armour, but also took to buying or making both themselves, and the technological gap between them and the Teutonic Order would narrow. The constant pressure also forced the fractious Lithuanians to accept the growing authority of the Grand Duke. Nevertheless, the Grand Dukes still needed to find new lands and resources with which to placate local chieftains and reward personal vassals. This meant that, while still fighting the Teutonic Order, they also launched campaigns in the lands of the Rus', bringing new principalities under their dominion. Meanwhile, the Ordensstaat consolidated its grip on Prussia and also, with the crusades to the Holy Lands now a thing of the past, they found themselves attracting growing numbers of foreign knights eager to join their campaigns against the 'heathens' of Lithuania.

A sign of the increasing sophistication of the Lithuanian state was the construction of Kaunas Castle. While first mentioned in surviving written records in 1361, it was completed perhaps ten years earlier, making it the oldest brick-built castle in the country. It was a crucial link in a defensive chain of fortifications defending Lithuania's western frontier, stretching from Žemaitija to the upper reaches of the Nemunas River. Indeed, it blocked a potential invasion route whereby the Teutonic Order could strike down through the lower reaches of the Nemunas river basin and into the heart of the Grand Duchy. As such, it would be a regular target for crusader attacks, but they were often hindered by a lack of siege engines and the time and

Found at Tannenberg Castle near Seeheim-Jugenhein in Germany, this steel gauntlet for the right hand dates from *c.*1380. (Sepia Times/ Universal Images Group via Getty Images)

manpower necessary to stage a lengthy siege. In 1361, however, Grand Master Winrich von Kniprode decided that Kaunas Castle had to be destroyed, both to prevent it from limiting the Teutons' scope for their raids and also as a symbolic blow against the 'heathens'. Besides which, at the time Kęstutis, duke of Trakai and co-ruler of Lithuania, was in crusader hands, and was imprisoned in Ordensburg Marienburg. This seemed the right moment to capitalize on the Lithuanians' presumed confusion and dismay.

In March 1361, Kęstutis – along with his brother and co-ruler Algirdas, and his son Patrikas – had launched a raid that managed to take and destroy the Teutonic Order's *Ordensburgen* of Eckersberg (Okartow) and Johannisburg (Pisz). As they were returning home, however, a force of knights that was, ironically, returning from a failed expedition of its own against Lithuania, came on their encampment near Ublik (Wobel) lake. They took the Lithuanians by surprise, and the 60-year-old Kęstutis was captured, although legend has it that he dispatched the first two knights who came up against him. It is a mark of the way that the crusade was by now as much a political and even commercial venture as a religious one, that once Kęstutis was imprisoned in the Ordensstaat's imposing headquarters in Ordensburg Marienburg, ransom negotiations began. Two successive rounds of haggling failed, as the Teutonic Order's price was too high. After six months in crusader hands, however, Kęstutis was able to escape alongside his servant Alfas, apparently by boring through the outer wall of the castle and then riding away, disguised as Teutonic

Knights. Given that the wall in question was 3m thick, and horses and the mantles of knights were not habitually left lying around the countryside, it seems likely that bribery or some backroom political deal was involved.

It was a mark of the importance von Kniprode put in this operation, that it was *Ordensmarschall* Henning Schindekopf, *Komtur* of Königsberg, who in the summer of 1361, led a force through the lands of the Sudovians, towards Kaunas. This was just a reconnaissance, however, and while Henrik von Neuhausen launched a feint to the south, Henrik von Schöningen, *Komtur* of Ragnit, led a group of experienced craftsmen to assess the nature of the defences of Kaunas Castle (Kuncevičius 2004: 223). As it was, they could not cross the Nemunas, and so could gather only partial intelligence.

This panoramic view of the modern-day city of Kaunas on the Nemunas River clearly shows the breadth of the river. (Julian Nyča/Wikimedia/CC BY-SA 4.0)

The construction of fortresses such as Kaunas Castle reflected the growing power of the Grand Duchy of Lithuania. (DEA/W. BUSS/Getty Images)

The siege of Kaunas, March–April 1362

MAP KEY

1 2 March: Grand Master Winrich von Kniprode and *Ordensmarschall* Henning Schindekopf muster a powerful force at Insterburg.

2 13 March: Having disembarked below Kaunas, the crusader army reaches Kaunas Castle and immediately begins to establish siegeworks.

3 28 March: Two weeks into the siege, the Livonian Order forces under Master Arnold von Vietinghof arrive.

4 30 March: Soon after the Livonian Order forces arrive, so too does a Lithuanian relief force, under Kęstutis and Algirdas.

5 16 April: Sections of the castle's inner walls collapse and the Teutonic Order's forces launch an assault. They are met by a desperate sally, as Vaidotas and his remaining men seek to cut their way free or at least sell their lives as dearly as possible. The Lithuanians are defeated and the survivors taken prisoner.

6 17 April: The Lithuanian relief force marches away, and the Teutonic Knights and their allies celebrate mass inside the ruins of the castle.

Battlefield environment

Dominating the confluence of the Nemunas and Viliya rivers, Kaunas Castle was built on a relatively narrow, flat strip of land between them on which previous wooden stockades and forts had stood for a century (the first settlements date back to the Iron Age). By contrast with these relatively simple earlier structures, the castle the Teutonic Order faced was a much more formidable fortress. It was an irregular rectangle of double red-brick walls on stone foundations, the walls enclosing an area of some 5,200 square metres, surrounded by a broad but shallow moat (the depth of water was likely no more than 1.5m). The walls were brick facings on a core of rock and rubble for strength and ease of construction and although many modern representations show the walls entirely surrounded by wooden, covered fighting galleries from which the defenders could rain arrows and stones down upon attackers, archaeological evidence suggests they only topped part of the walls, possibly because the fortification had not been entirely finished. The total height of the walls was around 9m, with the fighting galleries adding another 2.5–3m, and their width was about 2.5m. The outer defences were overlooked by circular- and square-base towers housing storerooms and barracks, between which were a variety of wooden structures, which would prove all too susceptible to incendiaries during the siege. In many ways, it was essentially comparable with many Teutonic Order castles. Although large enough for a castle and the eventual Teutonic siegeworks, the fact that the battle was taking place on a strip of land between two broad and fast-flowing rivers proved crucial, in that it allowed the attackers to fortify the neck of the strip and thus ensure that the Lithuanian relief army had no opportunity to lift the siege.

Symbolic of the growing sophistication of the Grand Duchy and the resources available to the Grand Duke, Kaunas Castle was an impressive red-brick construction that has been reconstructed since the original destruction of the fortress by the Teutonic Order. (Pudelek/Wikimedia/ CC BY-SA 3.0)

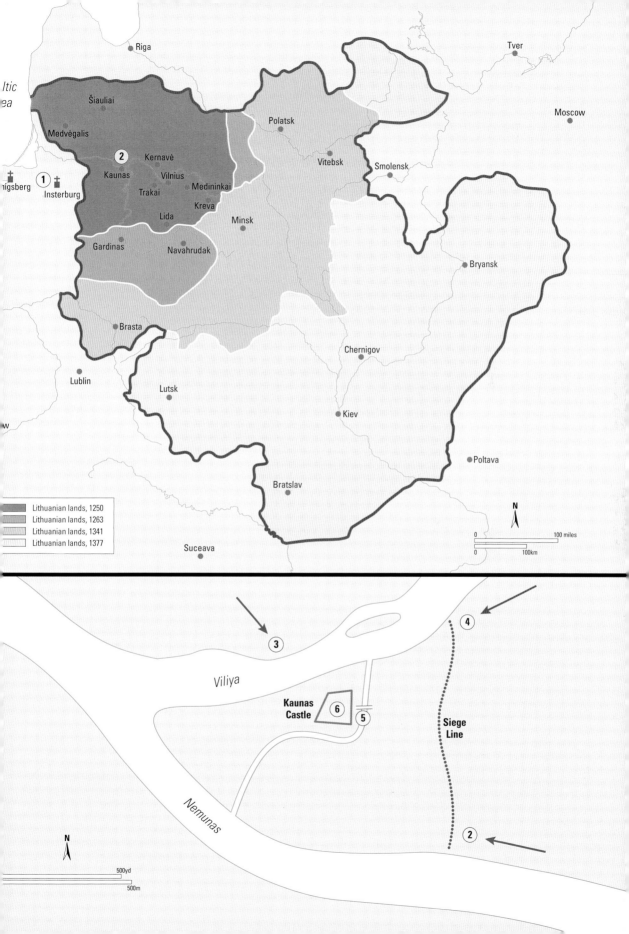

Lithuanian lands, 1250
Lithuanian lands, 1263
Lithuanian lands, 1341
Lithuanian lands, 1377

Itic
ea

Riga

Šiauliai

Medvėgalis

Polatsk

Tver

Moscow

(2)

Kernavė

Vitebsk

Smolensk

Kaunas

Vilnius

(1)

nigsberg

Insterburg

Trakai

Medininkai

Kreva

Lida

Minsk

Gardinas

Navahrudak

Bryansk

Brasta

Chernigov

Lublin

Lutsk

Kiev

w

Bratslav

Poltava

N

0   100 miles
0   100km

Suceava

N

Viliya

(3)

(4)

Kaunas
Castle

(6)

(5)

Siege
Line

(2)

Nemunas

N

500yd

500m

INTO COMBAT

While claims as to the strength of the castle garrison range up to 3,500, archaeological studies suggest a figure closer to 350 (Kuncevičius 2004: 223), although there were also at least as many servants and the like, who would nevertheless have been pressed into martial labour, whether as levies or in dousing fires and fetching ammunition. In any case, the bulk of the soldiers were seasoned fighting men, led by Kęstutis's son, Vaidotas. They had reason to feel confident: when the fighting galleries were included, the castle's walls were over 11m high, in part faced with clay, behind a moat.

That being said, von Kniprode wanted this to be a demonstration of the Teutonic Order's power. Originally, he had planned a winter assault, but the season proved unusually mild and not propitious for a major operation. As a result, it was pushed back to spring, when the crusaders could sail up the Nemunas, bypassing many of the Lithuanian forts and garrisons along the way. Von Kniprode and Schindekopf mustered a powerful force at Ordensburg Insterburg (near modern-day Chernyakhovsk, Russia), near Königsberg. It included the banners of Elbing, Christburg, Balga, Brandenburg, Insterburg, Ragnit and numerous other commanderies, as well as Bartholomew von Radam, Bishop of Semba (Samland), with his own forces, Grand Commander Wolfram von Baldersheim, and a contingent of Livonian Order knights under their Master, Arnold von Vietinghof. Furthermore, the Teutonic Order's army was supplemented by a substantial force of guest knights from England, Italy and Germany. This was a sizeable force, numbering perhaps 3,000–4,000 fighting men, as well as a large train of servants and specialists. While the former contingent was relatively heavily weighted towards knights, von Kniprode made sure the specialists included a full complement of military engineers, including Markvard, a master carpenter from Marienburg, and Matthias of Königsberg.

The crusader army disembarked below Kaunas, reached the castle on 13 March and immediately beginning to establish siegeworks. This work was conducted in a very professional manner. First, the crusaders built their own ring of ramparts and fortifications around the castle; then they dug a ditch from the Nemunas to the Viliya rivers. The aim was to create a moat dividing the castle and the besieging army's position from the mainland, in case of an attempt by the Lithuanians to lift the siege. Along this moat, they built a fence of sharp wooden stakes. Next, Markvard turned to constructing catapults and larger trebuchets to batter the castle's walls. Once they were in action, the Teutonic Order's craftsmen were put to work building siege towers that could be pushed up to the walls, and ladders.

Von Posilge's *Chronik des Landes Preussen* (*Chronicle of the Prussian Lands*) claims that they also had *Lothebuchszen*, crude arquebuses shooting lead bullets, but not *groszin Steynbuchszen*, or larger guns firing stone balls (Hecht 1914: 41). This is unlikely, however. Not only have there been no archaeological finds to support this contention, but the first mention of firearms in the Teutonic Order's own inventory books comes from 1374, when three were mentioned at Leipe (Lipienek). Furthermore, the chronicles of Wigand of Marburg only make reference to firearms during expeditions to Lithuania in the 1380s and 1390s. They hardly needed them,

not least because of the great disproportion between the two sides, especially when, two weeks into the siege, the Livonian forces under von Vietinghof arrived. Von Kniprode's concern, however, was that as the siege dragged on, a Lithuanian relief army would be able to encircle the attackers. This was a realistic threat. The crusaders had expected Kęstutis himself still to be in the castle, but although he had been there, he had recently left, apparently to gather an army to repel the crusaders' attack. Soon after the Livonians arrived, so too did a Lithuanian relief force under the command of Kęstutis and Algirdas.

One of the great debates about the battle is quite why the Lithuanian relief force never tried to engage. Indeed, some historians have even argued that the lack of such a battle means that Kęstutis and Algirdas must actually not have been there. In fact, these claims essentially run counter to the evidence and are rooted more than anything else in a reluctance to accept that a relief force would have stood by and seen Kaunas Castle fall, especially given Vaidotas's presence. Indeed, Wigand of Marburg recounted that Kęstutis actually parlayed with von Kniprode, claiming that 'if I were in the castle, you would never take it' (quoted in Hirsch 1863: 48). When von Kniprode then genially invited Kęstutis to join the besieged defenders, albeit accompanied only by his personal retinue, the Lithuanian demurred, realizing it would simply trap him there, too.

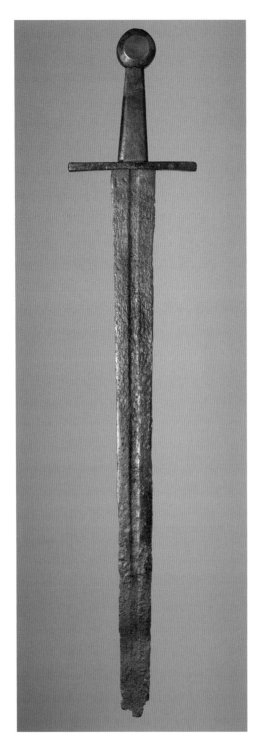

Dating from *c.*1350, this German sword has a 63cm blade. (Sepia Times/Universal Images Group via Getty Images)

The real answer is that the Teutonic army was both still larger and also by then solidly emplaced. For the Lithuanians to have attacked would have required them to launch an assault along a narrow, flat strip of land between the Nemunas and Viliya rivers, over the moat and palisade that had been built, and all amid a hail of arrows and crossbow bolts. Then, they would have smashed against more wooden palisades, overlooked by elevated firing positions, all built far enough away from the castle walls to prevent the risk of being caught by an unexpected sally by the defenders. Pragmatism triumphed.

Meanwhile, the siege artillery hammered away at the walls of the castle, while engineers began undermining them. The moat was filled with masonry, earth and wood. By 10 April, the outer walls had largely collapsed as a result of the military engineers' efforts, and the artillerymen began turning their attention to the inner walls and the buildings inside the castle, battering them with stones and hurling clay pots of flaming pitch to set light to wooden roofs and structures. Siege towers were rolled forward so that soldiers could take the tops of the walls, but the defenders were largely able to fend them off with logs, while raking them with arrows. It could not be long, however, and on 16 April, the eve of Easter Sunday, sections of the inner walls collapsed and the Teutonic forces launched an assault. They were met by a desperate sally, as Vaidotas and his remaining men of the garrison sought to cut their way free or at least sell their lives as dearly as possible.

The defenders had maintained their morale remarkably well considering the hopelessness of their position. Wigand of Marburg, for all that he was a herald of the Teutonic Order, was generous in his praise: 'the idolaters, attacked day and night, could not breathe a sigh of relief, but they defended themselves fiercely to the misfortune of the Christians' (Hirsch 1863: 58). Vaidotas proved to be an able and inspirational leader and also a doughty fighter. One story is that in that final sally, his shield was cleaved in two by a Teutonic Knight whom he then cut down, so he picked up another shield from a warrior from Vilnius, and then had to scavenge yet a third when that too was shattered by an enemy's mace.

As it was, only 36 of the defenders survived the siege and the final battle, including Vaidotas, who was taken prisoner. He was apparently treated honourably, and later released, because in 1365 he was made co-ruler with

his brother Tautvilas of the town of Navahrudak (Novogrudok). Nevertheless, this was the end of the battle. The Lithuanian relief force marched away, and the Teutonic Knights and their allies celebrated mass inside the ruins of the castle on Easter Sunday, 17 April 1362.

Christian chroniclers give the number of Lithuanian dead at around 2,000, although Wigand of Marburg, writing later, inflates the figure to a much less plausible 3,500, while claiming that while 600 fell in battle, the rest died in the flames of the burning castle. The former is credible. As for the Teutonic Knights and their allies, although Wigand of Marburg says only 200 fell, the true figure appears to be closer to 600, of whom 200 died in the final assault. According to Herman von Wartberge's *Chronicon Livoiale* (*Livonian Chronicle*), only seven full knights died, along with 20 of the guest knights (Strehlke 1863: 75). This ratio would reflect not the proportions of full knights and guest knights present, but the way the latter often had more to prove and would compete to demonstrate their bravery.

This was one of the most dramatic Teutonic victories of the whole crusade. Even in the lands of the Rus', chronicles from the city of Tver noted the fall of Kaunas Castle and the capture of Kęstutis's son. The Lithuanians smarted at the destruction of their newest and most advanced fortress. According to popular legend, Kęstutis's son Vytautas – who would have been just 11 years of age at the time, but went on to become one of Lithuania's greatest leaders – vowed, as he watched the castle burn, to dedicate his life to defeating the Teutonic Order.

Endgame at Kaunas Castle

On 16 April 1362, as the collapse of Kaunas Castle's inner walls makes a Teutonic assault both inevitable and irresistible, the remaining defenders of the castle launch one last, doomed sally. They are led by their captain, Vaidotas, who bears a shield he has had to take from a fallen ally, and while they are fighting valiantly, they are massively outnumbered. Vaidotas himself will manage to defeat the Livonian Order Sword-Brother trying to block his path, but this delays him long enough that he will be surrounded and subdued. A few Lithuanian archers and crossbowmen are still defending the walls, but as attackers swarm up siege ladders, it is just a matter of time until the defenders are overwhelmed. Meanwhile, catapults continue to launch balls of flaming resin into the inner precincts of the castle, igniting the last wooden buildings still standing.

Kaunas Castle itself was ruined by the siege and then the Teutonic Order's comprehensive slighting of it – the deliberate destruction of all that remained standing. The site was left abandoned, with the Lithuanians later building New Kaunas Castle further downstream, at the mouth of the Nevėžis River. This castle became the target of new attacks, and in 1369 the Teutons captured it, too. In 1384, Grand Master Konrad Zöllner von Rotenstein built a new castle of his own, Marienwerder (Kwidzyn), on the island in front of the old site, but as if to emphasize the degree to which this was a perennially contested location, the Lithuanians in turn captured the castle that same year. Only after the battle of Grunwald in 1410 and the decisive reversal of the Teutonic Order's fortunes, did the region lose its strategic importance and the city of Kaunas could grow in peace.

The memory of Vaidotas and his command of the defence of Kaunas Castle during the siege is marked by this commemoration stone at the modern-day castle. (Vilensija/Wikimedia/CC BY-SA 3.0)

Grunwald

1410

BACKGROUND TO BATTLE

In 1385, the ambitious Grand Duke Jogaila of Lithuania agreed to marry Queen Jadwiga of Poland in the Union of Krewo, entering into a dynastic marriage that required his conversion to Christianity. Having been baptized, he was crowned King Władysław II Jagiełło of Poland (r. 1386–1434). The Grand Duchy of Lithuania and the Kingdom of Poland remained distinct, but were held together by this personal union. Lithuania itself formally converted to Christianity in 1386, although paganism had been in decline there for years. Jogaila moved his seat to the Polish capital Kraków and his cousin Vytautas became his regent and Grand Duke in Lithuania.

Ostensibly, this would end any rationale for the crusades and, indeed, much of the very purpose of the Ordensstaat. Deep enmities and individual and institutional self-interest do not dissipate so easily, however, and the conflict had really become one of politics and economics as much as anything else. The Grand Master of the Teutonic Order at the time, Konrad Zöllner von Rotenstein, along with the king of Hungary, Sigismund of Luxembourg (r. 1387–1437), publicly challenged the conversion – or specifically Jogaila's sincerity – in a papal court. There was, after all, territory in question: Lithuania still disputed the Teutonic Order's control of Žemaitija, and Poland's stretches of Dobrzyń Land and the city of Gdańsk (Danzig). The Teutonic Order also feared the new union had designs on the trade revenues they had gained from their control of the lower stretches of the Nemunas, Vistula (Weichsel) and Daugava (Düna) rivers.

When the Samogitian Lithuanians revolted again in May 1409, Prussian forces were forced to withdraw from the region. When the Teutonic Order threatened to attack in response, Poland and Lithuania stood with the

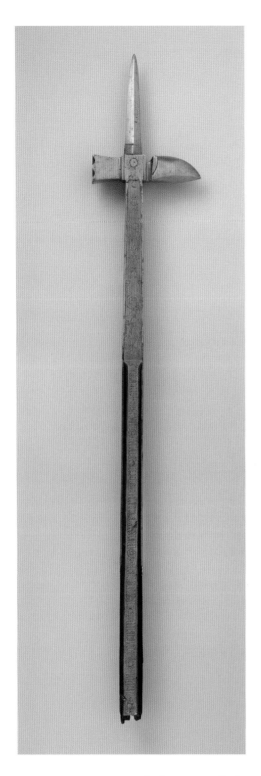

This German war hammer dates from the 15th century. (Heritage Art/Heritage Images via Getty Images)

Samogitians, raising the risk of an invasion of Prussia in response. Teutonic Order Grand Master Ulrich von Jungingen feared a war on two fronts and, in an attempt to pre-empt this risk, he declared war against Poland on 6 August. Polish ambassador Archbishop Mikołaj Kurowski had, after all, warned him that any attack on Lithuania would inevitably mean war with Poland. Rather than take this as a warning not to attack, von Jungingen decided he had to knock Poland out of the war quickly, such that either Lithuania would then back down, or the Teutonic Order's forces could be concentrated against it.

At first, the Teutonic Order had surprise and momentum on its side. The border fortress of Dobrzyń (Golub) had been a bone of contention between the Teutonic Order and Poland for almost two centuries, and had most recently been granted to the Teutonic Order by Jogaila and then bought from it by Poland. The fortress quickly fell to a crusader army using bombards in August 1409. The town and castle of Bobrowniki (Beberen) were taken after a longer siege, as well as the city of Bidgoscha (now rendered as Bydgoszcz, and called Bromberg in German), as the Teutonic army marched down the Vistula, raiding parties burning fields and sacking smaller towns.

A Polish counter-attack retook Bydgoszcz, but could push no further. In Samogitia, the rebels attacked Ordensburg Memel (Klaipėda Castle), but von Jungingen had recently had it refortified, and it held. Neither side was prepared to escalate the conflict, but nor was either party content, so they called a truce on 8 October and turned to King Wenceslaus IV of Bohemia (r. 1378–1419) to mediate. Known, perhaps a little unfairly, as 'the Idle', Wenceslaus IV was a man of great learning but precarious position, and the expectation was that he would delay any ruling and fudge the outcome. After all, both sides considered this as simply a chance to prepare for a resumption of hostilities when the truce came to its scheduled end on 24 June 1410.

In fact, Wenceslaus IV, keen to replenish his coffers, set about monetizing the opportunity. In return for the substantial sum of 60,000 florins, he gladly declared that while the Teutonic Knights had to return Dobrzyń Land to Poland, Samogitia was rightly the Teutonic Order's. Meanwhile, the Order was looking for allies. It dipped further into its substantial treasury to line up King Sigismund of Hungary, spending as much as 300,000 florins to get him to sign on to an agreement of mutual assistance. Sigismund then acted as their proxy in reaching out to Grand Duke Vytautas and encouraging him to claim the crown of Lithuania for himself, with the Ordensstaat's support. Vytautas demurred, but was himself secretly negotiating a separate truce with the Livonian Order, whose relationship with the main Teutonic Order had become increasingly strained.

There was little doubt that there would be a war: the only question was when, and who would strike the first blow. Von Jungingen anticipated that the Polish and Lithuanian armies would strike along two separate axes of attack. Although his total force lacked the Livonian Order's knights, he nevertheless had an impressive host of perhaps 30,000 men at his disposal. Of those, about half were Teutonic Order troops, a mix of knights and half-brothers, as well as Prussian cavalry and infantry levies. The rest were made up of 'pilgrims' – guest knights and their retinues – and mercenaries. From Sigismund of Hungary, von Jungingen received a force of 200 knights and Wenceslaus IV, always happy to play both sides off against each other for his own profit, had allowed the Teutonic Order to contract several hundred experienced Bohemian mercenaries, even as he allowed others to be hired out to Jogaila. The Teutonic Order also engaged some Genoese crossbowmen to provide additional ranged striking power.

Grand Duke Jogaila of Lithuania, otherwise known as King Władysław II Jagiełło of Poland, is depicted in this detail from a late-15th-century triptych in Wawel Cathedral, Kraków. (Unknown/ Wikimedia/Public Domain)

Von Jungingen and his senior commanders concurred that the Lithuanians would strike at the closest major target, Ragnit (Ragainė; modern-day Neman, Russia), opening up the prospect of then striking deeper into Prussia, while the Poles would march along the course of the Vistula towards Danzig on the Baltic coastline, so as to split the Teutonic Order's forces. Hence, while he kept substantial garrisons at Ragnit, Rhein (Ryn), Lötzen (Giżycko) and Memel (Klaipėda), he concentrated his forces around Schwetz (Świecie), with an eye to being able to pivot to meet one attack at a time.

Von Jungingen was wrong, however. In December 1409, Jogaila and Vytautas had agreed that they would combine their forces into a single host and rather than gnaw at the Teutonic Order's *Ordensburgen*, instead

The 13th-century Ordensburg Marienburg (Malbork Castle), the largest castle in the world when measured by land area, was Jogaila's true objective, yet remained beyond his grasp. (Michal Fludra/ NurPhoto via Getty Images)

strike directly for its capital, Marienburg (Malbork). While raids into the crusaders' border marches helped keep the defenders believing they faced threats from multiple directions, the Polish and Lithuanian armies began to muster at the town of Czerwińsk, on the northern bank of the Vistula, almost equidistant between Warsaw and the Prussian border. This was an impressive force. According to the *Chronik des Landes Preussen*, Jogaila gathered Tatars, Lithuanians, Russians and Samogitians into a formidable host so large it defied description, supplemented by mercenaries hired from Christian lands such as Bohemia and Moravia (Urban 2018: 111–12). It is certainly true that Jogaila's army was characterized as much by its heterogeneity as its size. Polish soldiers from Greater Poland gathered in Poznań (Posen) to the west, under Zyndram of Maszkowice, while the contingent from Lesser Poland assembled in Wolbórz to the south. These were together perhaps as many as 18,000 men – knights, squires and footmen. On 24 June they were joined by Jogaila and two banners of Czech mercenaries from Moravia and Bohemia under the Moravian military leader Jan Sokol of Lamberk. Sokol was a partisan of Wenceslaus IV, who despite taking the Teutonic Order's gold was also happy to turn a blind eye to this venture. Sokol, supported by Jan Žižka, later to be military leader of the Hussite revolt, was appointed to

command the fourth Polish banner of St George, composed of 1,500 cavalry. By 27 June, the Polish army had reached Czerwińsk, where engineers were already busy constructing a mighty pontoon bridge across the 600m-wide Vistula, completing it on 30 June.

Meanwhile, the Lithuanian forces led by Vytautas had been on the way since 3 June, marching from Vilnius (Wilna) to Hrodna (Garten), where they met up with Ruthenian forces from the lands of the Rus' including three banners of mixed cavalry and foot from Smolensk under Jogaila's brother Lengvenis and even a force of Crimean Tatar cavalry (mainly horse-archers) from the Golden Horde, under the command of Jalal ad-Din, who would later become khan. Together, they numbered some 10,000–11,000 warriors, mostly horse, although they were typically stronger in lighter cavalry than the Poles, and more used to a fluid and mobile style of warfare. They reached Czerwińsk on 2 July and joined the Polish army, just as further reinforcements arrived, from the Duchy of Masovia-Warsaw. After a sermon from the Bishop of Płock in which he encouraged them to fight the enemy to the death, this massive host, numbering perhaps 36,000–39,000 men, began lumbering north towards Marienburg. On 9 July, just 15 days after the truce had expired, it crossed the border, singing the hymn *Bogurodzica* ('Mother of God').

MAP KEY

1 **May:** Teutonic Order forces concentrate near Schwetz.

2 **3 June:** A Polish feint musters near Bydgoszcz.

3 **20 June:** The Greater Polish army musters at Poznań.

4 **26 July:** The Lesser Polish army musters at Wolbórz.

5 **29 July:** The Lithuanian army crosses the Narew.

6 **1 July:** The Polish armies meet, south of Czerwińsk.

7 **2 July:** Lithuanian forces join with Polish armies.

8 **2 July:** Teutonic Order forces reach Kauernik.

9 **7 July:** A Polish feint draws a detachment of Teutonic Order forces westwards, away from the main offensive.

10 **8 July:** Polish–Lithuanian forces reach Budzyń.

11 **9 July:** Polish–Lithuanian forces assault Lautenburg.

12 **10 July:** Teutonic Order forces block the Polish–Lithuanian advance at Kauernik.

13 **12 July:** Polish–Lithuanian forces regroup at Wysoka.

14 **13 July:** Polish–Lithuanian forces assault Gilgenburg.

15 **15 July:** Teutonic Order and Polish–Lithuanian armies meet at Grunwald; the allies prevail.

16 **17 July:** Polish–Lithuanian forces take Allenstein.

17 **18 July:** Mohrungen surrenders to Polish–Lithuanian forces.

18 **21 July:** Heinrich von Plauen, *Komtur* of Schwetz, leads reinforcements to Marienburg and takes command of its defence.

19 **22 July:** Christburg surrenders.

20 **25 July:** Polish–Lithuanian forces invest Marienburg: the siege lasts until 19 September.

Battlefield environment

The battle took place in a broad, gentle depression between the villages of Grunwald (Grünfelde), Tannenberg (Stębark) and Ludwigsdorf (Łodwigowo). The battlefield was broadly triangular, with the front line running along a north-east–south-west axis. The Teutonic Order's forces deployed across one of the points; the Polish–Lithuanians along the opposite broad face. Behind the latter was a lightly wooded rise, with a conical hill to the east, atop which Jogaila established his command post. Behind the crusaders' left flank, to the north-west, was a stretch of swampland, on the banks of which they established their rear encampment. On the other side was deep forest. Visibility was heavily constrained by the forests to the sides, and much of the ground was boggy and pocked with depressions, many of which had filled with groundwater to form small ponds.

The broad, flat battlefield provided ample scope for charge and counter-charge, in contrast with the woods around, as shown by this panoramic image. The modern monument to the battle in the distance, completed in 1963, is made up of 30m-high masts symbolizing Polish and Lithuanian banners, and a commemorative monolith. (Łukasz Niemiec/Wikimedia/ CC BY-SA 3.0 PL)

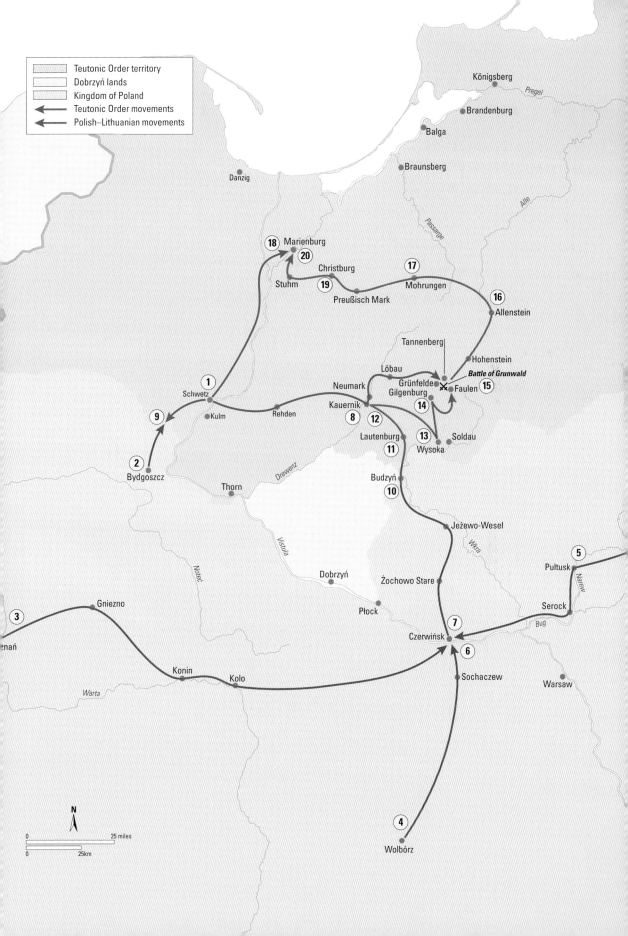

Teutonic Order territory
Dobrzyń lands
Kingdom of Poland
Teutonic Order movements
Polish–Lithuanian movements

Königsberg

Pregel

Brandenburg

Balga

Braunsberg

Alle

Danzig

Passarge

18 Marienburg **20**

Christburg **17** Mohrungen

Stuhm **19**

Preußisch Mark

16 Allenstein

Tannenberg

Hohenstein

Löbau

Battle of Grunwald

1 Grünfelde

Neumark Gilgenburg Faulen **15**

Schwetz Kauernik **14**

9 Kulm **8** **12**

Rehden Lautenburg **13** Soldau

2 Wysoka

Bydgoszcz Drewenz **11**

Thorn Budzyń

10

Vistula

Jeżewo-Wesel

Wkra

5

Notec Dobrzyń Żochowo Stare Pultusk

Gniezno Serock

Płock Narew

3 Czerwińsk Bug

...nań **7**

6

Konin Kolo Sochaczew Warsaw

Warta

N

0   25 miles

0   25km

4

Wolbórz

INTO COMBAT

At first, the Teutonic Order had no idea of the Polish–Lithuanian attack. As von Posilge recounts, the veteran Hungarian envoys Nicholas II Garai and Stibor of Stiborzieze were unable to dissuade the Polish king from launching his attack (Urban 2018: 112). A few days after the river crossing, the envoys alerted von Jungingen to the approaching army. Von Jungingen hurriedly revised his plans. Leaving behind Heinrich von Plauen, *Komtur* of Schwetz, with a reserve of 3,000 men, he moved the rest of his forces to Kauernik (Kurzętnik), the most obvious crossing over the Drewenz (Drwęca) River. There they quickly began to build field fortifications to block the river crossing, placing sharpened stakes along its banks and wooden stockades behind. The Polish–Lithuanian army arrived only to find the Teutonic forces ready for them. The two armies camped on their respective banks of the river, and Jogaila took counsel with his generals.

Seeing von Jungingen's army ready for him and strongly emplaced, Jogaila instead decided to swing east and follow the Drewenz upstream, to loop around its source and allow a clear run towards Marienburg. His hope was that the Polish–Lithuanian army could outmarch the Teutonic Order's army, but while Jogaila was used to the generally lighter, more nimble Lithuanian field forces, he was now commanding an army the size and composition of which made it no speedier than the crusaders. Jogaila's men bypassed the town of Soldau (Działdowo), with its Ordensburg castle, but the Order's army was following them, crossing the river near Löbau (Lubawa) and continuing the race eastwards.

According to von Posilge, von Jungingen was driven to try to end this war of manoeuvre by a terrible massacre that Jogaila's forces visited on 13 July upon the village of Gilgenburg (Dąbrówno) that lay in their path; the Polish king's men did not dare to cross the Drewenz, instead seizing Gilgenburg, mistreating and murdering its population and desecrating its churches (Urban 2018: 116). It seems beyond doubt that Gilgenburg was indeed burned down and looted by the invaders, but the anecdotal evidence for a general massacre rests purely with crusader sources and is very similar to other accounts of alleged 'heathen' atrocities – regardless of the fact that this was a predominantly Christian army. After all, accounts of the time are often formulaic, with certain classic elements such as enemy atrocities and telling omens. For example, Polish accounts suggest that their sentries that night saw a vision of a king defeating a monk on the surface of the moon, which was interpreted as a favourable sign.

What is beyond doubt is that the Teutonic Order's forces did pick up their pace, motivated by their anger and indignation (Urban 2018: 116), and on 15 July arrived in the vicinity of the village of Grünfelde (Grunwald), close to where the epic clash between the two armies would take place. The Poles would later name the village after Grunwald, and the Lithuanians translated it from German as 'green forest' and thus call it the battle of Žalgiris. The Germans, however, named it for Tannenberg, 'fir hill', after another local village.

The Polish–Lithuanian troops had reached the banks of Lake Lauben (Lubien), just over 2km south-east of the Teutonic Order's encampment. Fog and heavy rain meant that neither side was aware of the other until the

next morning, which dawned bright and clear. Jogaila was heading to Mass when the first of a series of increasingly urgent messages reached him, alerting him to the proximity of the enemy. He continued to his devotions, however, charging Vytautas with assessing the situation.

Vytautas, in turn, became alarmed that the Polish army in particular was largely unready for battle. Despite his anxious and exasperated entreaties – 'Brother! This is the day of battle, not prayer!' (quoted in Turnbull 2003: 41) – it took some hours for Jogaila to begin to prepare for battle. In that crucial time, an early crusader attack could have proven devastating; but while von Jungingen had demonstrated considerable skill in marshalling his forces and intercepting the invaders, he proved less able to seize the moment. His soldiers, many of whom had spent the night on the move, stood arrayed in battle order, awaiting a move from the Polish–Lithuanian forces. As the sun rose, they sweltered in their heavy armour.

Von Jungingen was aware that he was outnumbered, with 27,000 men pitted against a force with at least 10,000 more, but he also knew that his forces were in the main more disciplined and heavily armoured. He felt his best chance of victory was to provoke the enemy into an attack such that he would have the advantage of the defence and then unleash his heavy cavalry in a devastating counter-attack. Hence, he squandered the initiative.

Little did von Jungingen know of Jogaila's slow morning routine, and the desperate efforts being made to get the Polish forces ready for battle. For more than three hours, the Teutonic Order's troops stood and waited, harried occasionally by Lithuanian and Tatar horse-archers. In what was at once a gesture to the chivalric traditions of the time and a desperate gambit

'Two Swords' (c.1909), by the Polish painter Wojciech Kossak (1856–1942), depicts the moment when von Jungingen tried to goad Jogaila and Vytautas into action by presenting them with the twin 'Grunwald Swords' and impugning their courage. (The Picture Art Collection/Alamy Stock Photo)

Ulrich von Jungingen

In many ways, Ulrich von Jungingen was born for the position of Grand Master of the Teutonic Order. Born in 1360 to the Swabian noble house of Jungingen, he and his older brother Konrad were younger sons and therefore would not succeed to the family title. Instead, they joined the Teutonic Order, in which they rose thanks to their zeal and status. Nevertheless, Konrad was the real prodigy, as adept a diplomat and strategist as a commander, and he was elected Grand Master by a unanimous vote of the Grand Chapter in 1393 at the age of just 38. Ulrich benefited from his brother's patronage and became *Komtur* of Balga in 1396, and *Ordensmarschall* in 1404, a position he combined with the role of *Komtur* of Königsberg. He faced successive Samogitian risings, which he suppressed with a heavy hand, along with some judicious corruption of some of their leaders.

When Konrad died after a long illness in 1407, he reportedly warned his colleagues against choosing his hot-headed and unsubtle brother as a successor, even calling him a fool. Nevertheless, in some ways Konrad had simply been too successful and the name of von Jungingen had become talismanic. Ulrich was duly elected as Konrad's successor. Ulrich was active, forceful and determined, but his contempt for the Lithuanians and Samogitians alike was all too evident, and the rather wilier Grand Duke Vytautas happily stirred up trouble on his doorstep to provoke him. Perhaps wanting to demonstrate himself to be a greater Grand Master than his brother at least in this, Ulrich became increasingly determined to regain Dobrzyń Land, the territory Konrad had ceded to Poland in the name of peace, and this would lead inexorably to war and his own death. Ulrich von Jungingen was undoubtedly a skilled and fearless warrior and also an inspirational commander on the field, but this was a time when the Teutonic Order needed someone with a cool head and a mind able to think several steps ahead – two assets he decidedly lacked.

to spur Jogaila into action, von Jungingen sent heralds to Jogaila. According to the admittedly partial Polish historian Jan Długosz, whose account was written several decades after the battle, the heralds bore two plain swords and a mocking message for Jogaila and Vytautas (Mikos 1999: 321). The message offered the swords in an effort to bolster Jogaila's courage, so that he would stand and fight rather than continue hiding from the Teutonic Order's forces; moreover, von Jungingen offered to withdraw and fight at a place of Jogaila's choosing. In response, Jogaila said: 'We accept the swords you send us, and in the name of Christ, before whom all stiff-necked pride must bow, we shall do battle' (quoted in Turnbull 2003: 43). Długosz, however, recounts or invents a rather more florid response, having Jogaila invoke the Virgin Mary and his realm's patron saints – Stanislaus, Adalbert, Wenceslaus, Florian and Jadwiga – while leaving the choice of battlefield to the Almighty, placing his fate and that of his people in the hands of God in the hope that the battle would bring an end to the Order's relentless aggression (Mikos 1999: 320).

The Teutonic Order's forces did indeed withdraw from their previous positions, giving the invaders more room to manoeuvre. In this, von Jungingen's desperation to instigate an attack led him to a further tactical mistake. According to some sources, he had had his men dig concealed ditches as pit traps for enemy cavalry, but this withdrawal meant that the ditches no longer protected the Order's infantry lines. More to the point, it also extended the gaps between infantry and cavalry – such that they could not support each other as well – and while von Jungingen presumably intended this also to give his artillery a clear field of fire, it turned out that a brief rain shower had dampened their powder.

The twin 'Grunwald Swords' would go on to become marks of pride and symbols of the joint dynastic rule over Poland and Lithuania, but for now they helped to finally prod Jogaila into action. His battle line began to form. To the

Jogaila/Władysław II Jagiełło

Jogaila has the distinction of having been at once the last pagan Grand Duke of Lithuania and the first Lithuanian king of Christian Poland. Born a pagan, he converted to Christianity in 1386 and was baptized as Władysław in Wawel Cathedral in Kraków on 15 February 1386 as part of the dynastic alliance that saw him marry the young Queen Jadwiga, and be crowned King Władysław II Jagiełło of Poland. He then converted Lithuania itself to Christianity, and for all that this appeared to be nothing more than an act of pragmatic statecraft, or maybe precisely because of that, he proved publicly devout thereafter. On Queen Jadwiga's death in 1399, he became sole monarch in his own right, and the subsequent Jagiellonian dynasty of Poland was also the Gedimid dynasty of Lithuania, ruling both states until the death of Sigismund II Augustus, King of Poland and Grand Duke of Lithuania (r. 1548–72) in 1572. Under Jogaila/Jagiełło, the Polish–Lithuanian union state was the largest in Christendom, and this time is generally considered the beginning of Poland's Golden Age. While no physical coward, he was a statesman more than a warlord, as capable in managing the twin courts of Lithuania and Poland as he was in building wider alliances, and he continued to expand their power until his death in 1432.

left flank was the Polish army, under Zyndram of Maszkowice, with chivalric heavy cavalry to the fore. To the right were the lighter Lithuanian forces, under Vytautas. In the middle were the remaining allies and mercenaries, all in three lines of large, wedge-shaped formations 20 or more files deep.

The Teutonic Order's 27,000 men included fewer than 300 full Teutonic Knights, along with more knights raised from Prussian lands and also perhaps 200 guest knights, for a core of around 1,000 heavily armoured professional warriors. The bulk of them von Jungingen placed under Grand Marshal Friedrich von Wallenrode on the flank facing the Lithuanians. Von Jungingen's assumption was that the 'Saracens' could be counted on to attack more quickly and so be routed more easily, allowing von Wallenrode's mighty mailed fist of a force to swing round and smash into the enemy army from the flank.

As the Teutonic Order's forces re-formed, their artillerymen took the opportunity to start the hostilities, but such was the dampness of their powder, only two of the cannons actually fired, and with no effect. This was, nevertheless, enough to embolden Vytautas, who hoped to exploit the opportunity offered by the crusaders' temporary disarray. Rather than attacking the centre of the line, where the concealed ditches had been dug, he charged into the heavy forces directly in front of him, an act of what could be considered either extraordinary bravery or foolhardiness.

The two forces met 'and there was such a noise of breaking spears and the clash of metal swords that the roar was heard by people a good few miles away, as if a huge boulder was tumbling down' (quoted in Turnbull 2003: 48). The fighting was hard, but the Lithuanian light cavalry were largely outmatched by the Teutonic Knights, even though the Smolensk Russians and Vytautas himself received praise for their determination. After more than an hour's hard mêlée, the Lithuanians began to withdraw, and soon this became a general flight from the battlefield, despite Vytautas's own efforts to rally his men. Two of the three banners of Russians survived, however, and cut their way through to the rest of the army.

According to von Jungingen's plan, his men were then meant to regroup and roll up the right flank of the rest of the enemy forces. As was so often the case, however, knights became victims of their own aristocratic arrogance, especially the more numerous Prussian and guest knights. Perhaps almost a half of them pursued the retreating Lithuanians, caught up in the frenzy of the charge, even though the lighter Lithuanian cavalry could outrun them. Many of the knights found themselves isolated and vulnerable, while others wasted time scavenging for loot before giving any thought to moving against the Poles. Six banners did join the attack on the rest of the invading army, but later and fewer in number than had been intended. Von Wallenrode himself had fallen in the battle, and without him it proved impossible to execute the neat gambit von Jungingen had planned.

There has been much historical controversy over the Lithuanian retreat. Polish historians such as Długosz were happy to present the battle of Grunwald as a Polish victory, and claim that the Lithuanians were dispersed, but he makes no mention of the fact that they regrouped and later returned to the battlefield. More recently, there has been a revisionist school, starting with the historian Vaclaw Lastowski in 1909, which has presented this rather as a cunning Lithuanian ruse, a feigned retreat intended to lure the cream of the Teutonic Order's forces out of position (Baranauskas 2000: 25). After all, this was a classic tactic of the Mongols, and the Russians and thence the Lithuanians did learn this lesson in their years of fighting alongside or against them. In fairness, however, this tactic would usually have been carried out only by specific units, not a whole flank of an army, and rather more quickly re-formed into a counter-attack. While this interpretation may help spare some Lithuanian blushes, it is probably something of a stretch.

Either way, this did occupy a substantial portion of the Teutonic Order's best troops and also left a hole in their battle line. Meanwhile, however, the Polish forces on the right flank were coming under serious pressure. Grand Commander Kuno von Lichtenstein led a charge against the Poles, supported by those knights who had not chased the Lithuanians. The mêlée was fierce, especially as many of the Polish knights were equally as well and heavily armed and armoured as their Teutonic Order enemies, but the attackers made a particular effort to reach the royal banner of Kraków, not just because this was a symbol of national pride, but also because under it fought the flower of Polish chivalry. The standard-bearer, Marcin of Wrocimowice, was hard-pressed, and at one point dropped the banner, but the veteran knights surrounding him immediately seized the banner and raised it aloft (Mikos 1999: 322). The fighting went on.

The near-loss of his royal banner seems to have spurred Jogaila to action, however. Until this point, he was content essentially to watch, letting Vytautas in particular manage operational command on the battlefield. Now, Jogaila unleashed the second and third lines of his army. Under this new onslaught, the crusaders reeled, but the determination of the Teutonic Order's knights and the Czech and German guest knights fighting alongside them, ensured that the fighting continued (Mikos 1999: 323).

At this stage, the invaders seemed fully committed, however, so von Jungingen, from his hilltop command point, saw what he considered to be a vulnerability in their disposition and decided it was time to enter the fray. He had retained his own reserve of fully 16 banners of Teutonic Order troops, some 1,500 men, and he led them in a wide sweep round the scrum

(presumably to avoid the concealed ditches he had ordered dug) into the invaders' right flank, taking advantage of the gap left by the Lithuanians.

This was a desperate throw of the dice, but victory was still in von Jungingen's grasp. He aimed his charge squarely at Jogaila's position, reasoning that if Jogaila were killed or captured, then the allied forces would be demoralized and likely disperse. Jogaila himself, in stark contrast to his earlier passivity, would have met them in battle, had a Czech knight not – to his apparent anger – restrained his horse. While Jogaila's bodyguards crowded around him, and his personal banner was furled to avoid marking him out, the rest of the Polish army was too beleaguered to be able to spare any knights to join them. When the royal secretary, the young priest Zbigniew Oleśnicki, sought to persuade Mikolaj Kielbasa, commander of the court banner of royal favourites, to withdraw to protect Jogaila, he flatly refused, pointing out that turning tail and riding off to protect Jogaila would actually place Jogaila in more danger (Mikos 1999: 323).

Fortunately for Jogaila, however, it seems the Teutonic Knights became confused and, assuming Jogaila was in the thick of the battle, wheeled to join the grand mêlée at the centre of the battlefield. One exception was the Teutonic Knight Lupold von Kökeritz, who spied the king and charged

This 16th-century engraving accompanying a work by the Polish historian and chronicler Marcin Bielski (1495–1575) amply illustrates the bitter close-quarters no-holds-barred fighting that was the mêlée. (Universal History Archive/Getty Images)

This epic representation of the battle of Grunwald, by the Polish painter Jan Matejko (1838–93), dates from 1878. (National Museum in Warsaw/Wikimedia/Public Domain)

directly at him. Jogaila counter-charged, wounding him with his lance, and Oleśnicki then hit von Kökeritz with the broken butt of his lance, unhorsing the knight; the royal bodyguards, belatedly scrambling to the scene, quickly dispatched him.

Meanwhile, the arrival of the fresh Teutonic forces threatened to turn the tide in the main mêlée, which was becoming more and more like a confused and lethal brawl. At first, the Poles' morale wavered as they were assailed, but as much from desperation as determination, they steadied and continued their bloody work. At this stage, however, the battle took a new twist as Vytautas led back to the battle the remnants of the Lithuanians, whom he had managed to rally on the road to the village of Faulen (Ulnowo). They, in turn, rode headlong into the rear of the Teutonic forces, their *sudlice* polearms wreaking bloody revenge for their previous rout.

Von Jungingen's gamble had failed. His soldiers were outnumbered, the advantage of the charge had been lost, and in the vicious mêlée, his cavalry were all too vulnerable even to humble footmen, pulling horsemen from the saddle or stabbing horses with their spears. Von Jungingen chose the better part of valour and signalled a general retreat. He himself would not make it off the battlefield: as he tried to cut his way free and get back to Grunwald, he was killed, a lance thrust through his neck. According to Długosz, this was at the hands of Mszczuj of Skrzynno, a knight of the royal household, while the account in the *Cronica conflictus Wladislai regis Poloniae cum Cruciferis anno Christi 1410* (*A Chronicle of the Conflict of Władysław, King of Poland, with the Crusaders, 1410 AD*), a contemporaneous account the Polish author of which is uncertain, states that it was Dobiesław of Oleśnica. Either way, this was the last straw for the crusaders, whose turn it was to rout.

They were harried by Polish forces, but especially lighter Lithuanian and Tatar horseman, who broke up any attempts to stand and rally. Some of the crusaders headed back to their camp, whether to find remounts or reclaim their goods, but there they were met by their own camp followers, many of whom had been press-ganged into service. They turned against their masters, whether for revenge or to be able to plunder the supply train themselves. Nevertheless, some of the surviving Teutonic Order forces tried to use the

This stirring painting by the Polish painter Tadeusz Popiel (1863–1913) dates from 1910, the 500th anniversary of the battle of Grunwald. (Fine Art Images/Heritage Images/ Getty Images)

supply train to form a *Wagonburg*, a defensive circle of wagons, but they were too few in number and too disorganized to hold the line, and the arriving Polish–Lithuanian forces made short work of this last line of defence.

By mid-afternoon, after ten hours of marching and fighting, the battle was over. The Teutonic Order's supply train was promptly looted, Długosz stating that several thousand wagons were plundered so thoroughly that no trace of them remained (Mikos 1999: 326). The great stock of barrels of wine quickly attracted the attention of the parched soldiers, such that Jogaila sternly ordered the barrels staved in, lest his men get insensibly drunk and therefore vulnerable to any unexpected counter-attack. The soldiers also found several wagons containing chains and fetters intended for their Polish captors in the wake of an inevitable Teutonic Order victory; in the event, the Order's hubris would mean that these shackles were put on their own leaders (Mikos 1999: 326). Many knights were indeed taken prisoner, including commanders such as Duke Kazimierz V of Pomerania and Duke Konrad VII the White of Oleśnica. They were held for ransom, but thousands of commoners and mercenaries were soon released. The Teutonic Order's losses, however, were startling. All told, of the 270 full brothers who marched to Grunwald, between 203 and 211 fell in battle, including the majority of its leadership: Grand Master Ulrich von Jungingen, Grand Marshal Friedrich von Wallenrode, Grand Commander Kuno von Lichtenstein, Treasurer Thomas von Merheim, Marshal of Supply Albrecht von Schwartzburg, and ten of the 20 *Komture* in the host. The highest-ranking officer who managed to escape was Werner von Tettinger, *Komtur* of Elbing. The envoys of King Sigismund of Hungary claimed the total casualties were 8,000 dead on both sides, but it is ambiguous as to whether this figure is for each side or in total. A papal bull from 1412 spoke of 18,000 dead Christians, which would imply the former.

Jogaila's original objective had been Marienburg, the seat of Ordensstaat power, and although he had won a startling and bloody victory over the Teutonic Order, he knew that this would not in itself destroy them as an institution. Nevertheless, the battle had taken its toll, and he needed to let

The atmospheric 'After the Battle of Grunwald: The Solidarity of the Northern Slavs' (1924), part of the Slav Epic cycle by the Czech painter Alfons (Alphonse) Mucha (1860–1939), conveys the carnage of the battle. (Fine Art Images/Heritage Images/Getty Images)

his army recover, with time to mourn and bury its dead, distribute its loot, and rest. Three days later, Jogaila's forces resumed their advance, albeit at a rather slower rate. This gave the Teutonic Order some time to regroup, under Heinrich von Plauen, *Komtur* of Schwetz, who hurriedly marched his 3,000 men from Schwetz to Marienburg and took command.

Meanwhile, Jogaila also dispatched contingents to Teutonic Order cities and castles. Many surrendered straight away, including Danzig, Thorn and Elbing, as well as the *Ordensburgen* of Christburg (Dzierzgoń), Hohenstein and Osterode (Ostróda), leaving just eight still under the Teutonic Order's control. This involved a dilution of Polish–Lithuanian forces, but Jogaila counted on Marienburg also falling quickly and easily. This proved to be a mistake, however. His army reached the Teutonic Order's fortress – then one of the most formidable in northern Europe – on 26 July. They found von Plauen defiant and ready for a lengthy siege, something the invaders manifestly were not. They were not simply exhausted and depleted by the battle of Grunwald, they also lacked an adequate siege train and would fall victim to an epidemic of dysentery. Von Plauen had also had the surrounding farmland and woods torched to deny the Polish–Lithuanian forces food and also the materials with which to build shelter and siegeworks.

Von Plauen's appeals for assistance were bearing fruit. In particular, Sigismund of Hungary and the Livonian Order were willing to send reinforcements, while Wenceslaus IV, in another show of astute statecraft, offered to lend von Plauen money with which to hire his own mercenaries. It is harder to know for sure whether the Hungarians and Bohemians were truly sending forces, but the Livonians, shamed by essentially sitting out von Jungingen's campaign thanks to their treaty with Jogaila, were certainly marching a force of at least 500 tough, fresh crusaders to von Plauen's relief.

By the end of August, Jogaila was facing increasing calls for him to withdraw, and he was running short of coin to pay his mercenaries. Vytautas led his Lithuanian forces home at the beginning of September, but Jogaila hung on until 19 September, before accepting defeat and heading home. Garrisons were left in the fortresses the invaders had seized, but they were too small to hold on in the face of a Teutonic Order counter-attack and, it is likely, had little incentive to do so in light of Jogaila's retreat. Most of the fortresses soon fell, with only four border fortresses – Nessau (Nieszawa), Rheden (Radzyń Chełmiński), Strasburg (Brodnica) and Thorn (Toruń) – remaining in Polish hands by the end of October.

Jogaila did stage one more, rather less expansive campaign that led to victory on 10 October over a small Teutonic army at Koronowo (Krone), a Polish town near Bydgoszcz that commanded strategic trade routes to Danzig and from Chełmno Land to Western Pomerania. In many ways, however, that battle itself was a metaphor for the current state of the wider war, in which the Polish–Lithuanian alliance may have had the advantage, but bitterness and exhaustion were almost stronger still. As Długosz asserted, no-one could recall so bitter a battle waged by two forces so equally matched, the deadlock broken only when a Polish horseman named as Jan Naszan toppled a Teutonic Order standard-bearer from his mount and captured his banner; this action precipitated a withdrawal by the Order's forces, as self-preservation outweighed shame and the Order's defeat became certain (Allan & Michael 1997: 400).

Both sides were spent, and they agreed to re-open negotiations. The Polish–Lithuanian alliance had essentially won the war, but they found it harder conclusively to win the peace. The Ordensstaat found a new Grand Master in von Plauen, who proved as capable a diplomat as a commander. It also found its scapegoat, Nikolaus von Renys, a Prussian of apparently Polish ancestry, who had argued for peace before the war. Nevertheless, at the battle of Grunwald it fell to him to bear the banner of the Culmerland contingent

A memorial was erected on this site in Kraków to commemorate the 500th anniversary of the battle of Grunwald, but it was destroyed by German forces during World War II. Rebuilt in 1976, it features King Władysław II Jagiełło of Poland (top), a Polish knight at one side and an anachronistically primitive Lithuanian warrior on another. (Mach240390/Wikimedia/ CC BY 4.0)

Jogaila could reach Marienburg – but he could not take it without time and, above all, proper siege artillery like this trebuchet. (Jebulon/Wikimedia/CC0 1.0)

in the Teutonic Order army. The claim that was made against von Renys was that at a crucial moment in the final mêlée, he lowered the banner, making it look as if he was signalling retreat, and that this led to their withdrawal. There is no evidence for this, but as a secular knight, a Prussian, and an alleged Polish sympathizer, he fitted the frame all too well. Denied even a trial, von Renys was beheaded in Graudenz (Grudziądz) in May 1411, and his male descendants were also killed – all in direct violation of the terms of the recently signed Peace of Thorn, which had banned the persecution of traitors and deserters after the battle. If anyone was to blame for the defeat, it was von Jungingen, a man whose strategic vision and diplomatic skills were not the equal of his valour, and who proved a Grand Master badly suited to an age when the Teutonic Order was facing a growing Polish–Lithuanian challenge and could no longer rely on the rallying cry of crusade against the 'heathen'.

Analysis

In 1266, the English philosopher and Franciscan friar Roger Bacon delivered a damning critique of the Teutonic Order's tactics in the Baltic Crusades, regarding them as counter-productively violent and driven not by a desire to convert, but a need to conquer:

> So the Saracens … become impossible to convert in many parts of the world, and especially Overseas and in Prussia and the lands bordering Germany, because the Templars and Hospitallers and the brothers of the Teutonic Order much disturb the conversion of infidels because of the wars which they are always starting, and because of the fact that they wish to dominate them absolutely. For there is no doubt that all the infidel nations beyond Germany would have been converted long ago, if it was not for the violence of the brothers of the Teutonic Order. The pagan race has many times been ready to receive the faith in peace after preaching, but those of the Teutonic Order do not wish to allow this, because they wish to subjugate them and reduce them to slavery. By subtle persuasions they have already deceived the Roman Church for many years. (Bridges 1900: 122)

While there clearly were extremely devout brothers, in terms of its grand strategy, the Ordensstaat did indeed not only overreach but miscalculate what a strategy which had worked in its own brutal fashion against the scattered Prussian tribes would do when used against the relatively unitary Lithuanian state. After all, whether it knew it or not, the Teutonic Order was in a battle against time to maintain its organization and technological advantage. Under the pressure of the Order's attacks, Lithuania was forced to modernize in both respects, such that it was then able to unite with Poland and, in the process, form a political force which would in time dominate north-central Europe and deliver a devastating blow to the Order, for all its undoubted strengths.

VOPLAUKIS

The Lithuanians had become used to raiding not just each other, but the Prussians and the Rus'. Sometimes they won, sometimes they lost, but essentially they tended to have the advantage against relatively poorly organized and divided enemies. In this context, it is hardly surprising that, once forced into a straightforward battle by von Plötzke's prediction of his movements, Vytenis was likely to lose. His defeat at Voplaukis, as one of the earliest engagements of the specifically Lithuanian Crusade, was important not just in its immediate consequences, but also as a learning experience on both sides.

By their incursions into the newly Christianized lands of Prussia, the Lithuanians helped ensure that the Teutonic Order would regard it as necessary to drive further eastwards along the Baltic coast, bringing crusade to these new upstarts. It also demonstrated that the Lithuanians could muster forces of a scale and competence able to raid deep into Ordensstaat lands and also move quickly enough that, without proper intelligence and preparation, it would be hard to bring them to battle. At that point, the Teutonic Knights were able to defeat the numerous but relatively poorly equipped Lithuanian raiders; the challenge was to fix them in place when they had the initiative.

As for the Lithuanians, Voplaukis likewise demonstrated starkly the power of the Teutonic Knights in a direct fight, regardless of who had the advantages of height and defence. Although the raid would remain the confrontation's primary expression, nevertheless this can be seen as the moment when the Lithuanians truly came to realize that they were not simply in an age of continual low-level rivalry, but now at war.

The triumphs of the Teutonic Order were often used to exalt German statehood and martial prowess, such as in 'Der deutsche Orden erstürmt Kauen' ('The German Order storms Kaunas'), a 19th-century representation that contrasts the pious but victorious knights with the barbaric Lithuanians – including Vaidotas on the left. (Adolf Ehrhardt/Wikimedia/Public Domain)

THE SIEGE OF KAUNAS

This realization would help drive the increasing centralization of the Lithuanian state and the mobilization of resources sufficient to begin to build modern, brick-built castles to try to limit the Teutonic Knights' strategic mobility and their capacity to raid into Lithuanian territory. This, in turn, limited the Lithuanians' own capacity to outmanoeuvre the Teutonic Order's forces. Although Kaunas did fall, and the Lithuanian relief army ultimately chose not to engage, the Lithuanians were closing the gap in military capacity and thinking with the crusaders.

The attack on Kaunas was a victory for the Teutonic Order, one which was won as much by their siegecraft and ability to sustain large forces in the field thanks to their well-organized logistics as the valour and

ferocity of their soldiers. The scale of this operation also demonstrated the degree to which the Ordensstaat was coming to think of this more like a war against an enemy state than, as was the case in Prussia, an episodic exercise in bringing their authority to local tribes.

Heavily armed and armoured re-enactors on horseback are pictured in action on the 607th anniversary of the battle of Grunwald. (Michal Fludra/NurPhoto via Getty Images)

GRUNWALD

After the Grand Duchy of Lithuania had finally converted to Christianity, as part of the dynastic alliance with Poland, the religious rationale for the wars would seem to have ended. Nevertheless, the Ordensstaat, unwilling to end the lucrative *Reisen* and abandon its hopes of controlling Lithuania, refused to accept this conversion. Arguably, this had become a struggle for political power in north-east Europe, only lightly veiled in the forms of crusade.

This refusal, however, failed properly to appreciate the fundamental shifts that had taken place in economic and military power. Lithuania was no longer a tribal union, and Poland was a rising regional power, whose chivalry – like many Lithuanian warriors – were as well equipped and trained as any Teutonic Knights. Furthermore, they were equally as able to attract allies and hire mercenaries, with a treasury as deep as that of the Teutons.

In this context, the climactic battle of Grunwald, which effectively ended the Baltic Crusades and led to the Teutonic Order's decline, was defined by a combination of numbers, tactics and luck. The larger numbers of Polish–Lithuanian soldiers were effectively offset by the higher aggregate quality and shorter supply lines of the Teutonic Order's forces, and in essence the two armies were using similar tactics. Thus, the outcome was decided as much as anything else by von Jungingen's impetuous nature and Vytautas's ability to rally the Lithuanians just in time. Had the Grand Master been Ulrich's brother Konrad, or Vytautas been less effective a commander than he was, things could have gone very differently.

Aftermath

Writing of the battle of Koronowo, fought on 10 October 1410, Długosz claimed that expert commentators deemed it even more significant than the battle of Grunwald, an importance underlined by the valour and hardiness displayed by the forces engaged (Allan & Michael 1997: 401). In practice, however, it was Grunwald that was a truly pivotal moment in late medieval European military history, not just one of the largest battles in medieval Europe, but also one that shifted the whole balance of power, as the new Polish–Lithuanian union became the dominant power in Central and Eastern Europe.

In the Peace of Thorn of February 1411, the Teutonic Order surrendered Dobrzyń Land to Poland and deferred any claims to Samogitia at least for the lifetimes of Jogaila and Vytautas. In practice, this proved easier to promise than enforce, and it would take another two wars, the Hunger War of 1414 and the Gollub War of 1422, before the Prussian–Lithuanian border would finally be fixed in the 1422 Treaty of Melno. The real cost to the Order was financial, with a substantial indemnity to be paid in silver in four annual instalments. Between buying allies and hiring men, von Jungingen had dipped heavily into the Order's coffers, and von Plauen had then had to spend more to save Ordensburg Marienburg. The Order thus had to resort to extreme measures, raising taxes, confiscating gold and silver from churches, and borrowing heavily. Danzig and Thorn both rose in revolt against the new taxes, and with Samogitia finally now officially Christian, the Order's capacity to attract paying guest knights and endowments declined dramatically. In a vicious circle, with its forces so heavily depleted after Grunwald and the other battles of the campaign, the Order had to hire mercenaries to suppress the revolts – mercenaries who themselves had to be paid, at the cost of more borrowing, and thus more tax.

The Treaty of Melno ended 225 years of war, but it also marked the start of an inexorable decline in the Teutonic Order. Rapacious tax demands,

Measuring 63.5cm by 34.9cm, this hand pavise (shield) dating from c.1450 bears the coat of arms of the Teutonic Order. (Artokoloro/Alamy Stock Photo)

rivalries within the Order's leadership and a wider economic crisis led to the formation in 1440 of the Preussischer Bund (Prussian Confederation) by an array of Prussian cities, noblemen and clerics. Formally protesting the Order's harsh and arbitrary policies, in practice it represented a nascent sense of Prussian identity and nationhood. As the lesser of two evils, in 1454, the Prussian Confederation formally petitioned to be allowed to join the Kingdom of Poland. This sparked the Thirteen Years' War (1454–66) between Poland and the Ordensstaat, a conflict that ended in another Teutonic defeat, and the Second Peace of Thorn of 1466.

The Teutonic Order surrendered swathes of lands to Poland, including what became the new Polish province of Royal Prussia. While the Order retained some portions of Prussia, it would lose even these in the Polish–Teutonic War (1519–21). Piece by piece, step by step, the German Order would retreat, on a long, slow, downhill path that would bring it to the present day, when it still survives but in radically different and unmilitary form.

Meanwhile, Lithuania was in many ways at its apogee. Vytautas would later become King of Lithuania after Jogaila's death on 1 June 1434, but he too died shortly thereafter. Both Polish and Lithuanian magnates intrigued against the union, but with the threatening rise of Muscovy to the east, Lithuania was forced into a closer relationship with Poland that came to look more like a takeover than a marriage. The result was the creation of the Polish–Lithuanian Commonwealth in 1569, through the Union of Lublin of the same year. Lithuania remained autonomous, with its own laws, currency and institutions, but in practice increasingly faced creeping 'Polonization'.

The Polish–Lithuanian Commonwealth remained a powerful force into the 17th century, but it faced an increasingly dangerous international situation, with the ascent of Sweden and Russia. While Commonwealth armies would take advantage of the Time of Troubles (1598–1613) before the installation of the Romanov dynasty briefly to occupy Moscow, the pendulum had swung. Vilnius had never fallen to a foreign invasion – until 1655, when it fell to a Russian army, after which Tsar Alexis of Russia (r. 1645–76) declared himself Grand Duke of Lithuania.

Jogaila may be a Lithuanian national hero, but Jagiełło is a Polish one, whose name has been carried abroad by the Polish diaspora. The King Jagiełło Monument in New York's Central Park features the fabled twin 'Grunwald Swords'. (CZmarlin/Wikimedia/CC BY-SA 4.0)

OPPOSING LEADERS

Grand Masters of the Teutonic Order

1198–1208	Heinrich Walpot von Bassenheim
1208	Otto von Kerpen
1208–09	Heinrich von Tunna
1209–39	Hermann von Salza
1239–40	Konrad von Thüringen
1240–44	Gerhard von Malberg
1244–49	Heinrich von Hohenlohe
1249–52	Gunther von Wüllersleben
1252–56	Poppo von Osterna
1256–73	Anno von Sangerhausen
1273–82	Hartmann von Heldrungen
1282–90	Burchard von Schwanden
1290–97	Konrad von Feuchtwangen
1297–1303	Gottfried von Hohenlohe
1303–11	Siegfried von Feuchtwangen
1311–24	Karl von Trier
1324–30	Werner von Orseln
1331–35	Lothar von Braunschweig
1335–41	Dietrich von Altenburg
1342–45	Ludolf König von Wattzau
1345–51	Heinrich Dusemer
1351–82	Winrich von Kniprode
1382–90	Konrad Zöllner von Rotenstein
1391–93	Konrad von Wallenrode
1393–1407	Konrad von Jungingen
1407–10	Ulrich von Jungingen
1410–13	Heinrich von Plauen

Rulers of Lithuania

1253–63	King Mindaugas
1263–64	Grand Duke Treniota
1264–67	Grand Duke Vaišvilkas
1267–69	Grand Duke Švarnas
1270–82	Grand Duke Traidenis
1282–85	Grand Duke Daumantas
1285–91	Grand Duke Butigeidis
1291–95	Grand Duke Butvydas
1295–1315	Grand Duke Vytenis
1316–41	Grand Duke Gediminas
1341–45	Grand Duke Jaunutis
1345–77	Grand Dukes Algirdas and Kęstutis (co-rulers)
1377–85	Grand Duke Jogaila
1386–1434	Grand Duke Jogaila/King Władysław II Jagiełło of Poland

Vilnius Castle. Much of the once-impressive castle that the Gedimids built for their capital has not survived, but Gediminas Tower still looks down over the capital. When Lithuania re-asserted its independence from the Soviet Union in 1988, its yellow, green and red national flag was symbolically flown from the tower. (© Mark Galeotti)

BIBLIOGRAPHY

Allan, Jane, ed. & Michael, Maurice, trans. (1997). *The Annals of Jan Długosz: A History of Eastern Europe from A.D. 965 to A.D. 1480, abridged*. Chichester: IM Publications.

Arndt, Wilhelm, ed. (1866). 'Annales canonici Sambiensis.' *Monumenta Germaniae Historica* vol. 18. Hanover: Scriptores.

Baranauskas, Tomas (2000). *Lietuvos valstybės ištakos*. Vilnius: Vaga.

Bridges, John Henry, ed. (1900). *The Opus Majus of Roger Bacon, volume 3*. Oxford: Clarendon Press.

Butterwick, Richard & Pawlikowska, Wioletta, eds (2021). *Social and Cultural Relations in the Grand Duchy of Lithuania: Microhistories*. Abingdon: Routledge.

Campbell, David (2015). *Templar Knight vs Mamluk Warrior*. Combat 16. Oxford: Osprey Publishing.

Chodyński, Antoni Romuald (2002). 'The preparations for war expeditions to Lithuania and Samogitia according to the Chronicle by Wigand of Marburg', *Fasciculi Archaeologiae Historicae* 15. Łódź: Instytut Archeologii i Etnologii PAN: 39–46.

Christiansen, Eric (1997). *The Northern Crusades*. Harmondsworth: Penguin. First published in 1980.

Fischer, Mary, ed. (2010). *The Chronicle of Prussia by Nicolaus von Jeroschin: A History of the Teutonic Knights in Prussia, 1190–1331*. Abingdon: Routledge.

Frost, Robert (2018). *The Oxford History of Poland-Lithuania: Volume I: The Making of the Polish-Lithuanian Union, 1385–1569*. Oxford: Oxford University Press.

Hecht, Kurt (1914). *Die Schlacht bei Rudau 1370*. Königsberg: Albertus-Universität.

Hirsch, Theodor, ed. (1863). *Die Chronik Wigands von Marburg. Originalfragmente, lateinische Uebersetzung und sonstige Ueberreste in Scriptores rerum Prussicarum*. Leipzig: Hirzel Verlag.

Kuncevičius, Albinas, ed. (2004). *Castella Maris Baltici 6*. Vilnius: Savastis.

Lindholm, David & Nicolle, David (2007). *The Scandinavian Baltic Crusades 1100–1500*. Men-at-Arms 436. Oxford: Osprey Publishing.

Markman, Kristina (2011). 'Tactics of Manipulation: A Revisionist Study of Gediminas and the Threat of Teutonic Invasion, 1315–1342', *Comitatus* 42.1: 115–33.

Markman, Kristina (2015). *Between Two Worlds: A Comparative Study of the Representations of Pagan Lithuania in the Chronicles of the Teutonic Order and Rus'*. Los Angeles, CA: UCLA Press.

Meyer, Leo, trans. (1876). *Die Livländische Reimchronik*. Paderborn: Schöningh.

Mikos, Michael, ed. (1999). *Polish Literature from the Middle Ages to the End of the Eighteenth Century: A Bilingual Anthology*. Warsaw: Constans.

Murray, Alan, ed. (2001). *Crusade and Conversion on the Baltic Frontier 1150–1500*. Abingdon: Routledge.

Murray, Alan, ed. (2009). *The Clash of Cultures on the Medieval Baltic Frontier*. Abingdon: Routledge.

Nicholson, Helen, ed. (1998) *The Military Orders Volume II: Welfare and Warfare*. Abingdon: Routledge.

Nicolle, David (2007). *Teutonic Knight: 1190–1561*. Warrior 124. Oxford: Osprey Publishing.

Norkus, Zenonas (2017). *An Unproclaimed Empire: The Grand Duchy of Lithuania: From the Viewpoint of Comparative Historical Sociology of Empires*. Abingdon: Routledge.

North, Michael & Kronenberg, Kenneth (2016). *The Baltic: A History*. Cambridge, MA: Harvard University Press.

Pluskowski, Aleksander (2012). *The Archaeology of the Prussian Crusade: Holy War and Colonisation*. Abingdon: Routledge.

Rowell, Stephen (1989). 'Lithuania and the West, 1337–41 – A question of sources', *Journal of Baltic Studies* 20.4: 303–26.

Rowell, Stephen (2014). *Lithuania Ascending: A Pagan Empire within East-Central Europe, 1295–1345*. Cambridge: Cambridge University Press.

Strehlke, Ernst, ed. (1863). *Chronicon Livoniae der Hermann von Wartberge*. Leipzig: S. Hirzel.

Turnbull, Stephen (2003). *Tannenberg 1410: Disaster for the Teutonic Knights*. Campaign 122. Oxford: Osprey Publishing.

Urban, William (2003). *The Teutonic Knights. A Military History*. London: Greenhill Books.

Urban, William (2018). *The Last Years of the Teutonic Knights: Lithuania, Poland and the Teutonic Order*. London: Greenhill Books.

Zikaras, Arolis (2017). *Battle of Saulė 1236*. Vilnius: Military Cartography Centre of the Lithuanian Armed Forces.

INDEX